The Theory
Highway Code \

This workbook contains **all the official ....**
answers as used in the UK theory test for car drivers. This Crown
copyright material is reproduced under licence from the Controller of
Her Majesty's Stationery Office (HMSO) and the Secretary of State
for the Environment, Transport and the Regions.

Published by:	Teaching Driving Limited Telephone No. (01977) 691818
Version:	2003/2004
ISBN:	0-9529035-6-3
Compiled and written by:	Paul McArdle and Val Wood
Graphic Design by:	Michael Bedford

The Theory Test CD-Rom ... made it easy

The ultimate learning tool for the theory test for car drivers

▶ Three theory test learning programmes
▶ Accurate theory mock test environment
▶ Hazard perception video explanations
▶ Accurate hazard perception mock test
▶ Interactive Highway Code
▶ Supplementary notes
▶ Learn to drive lesson briefs

Price £9.99

Call Freephone 0800 400 777 or visit www.LearnerDriving.com

Part 1 - Multiple Choice

Disk 1 contains all the official DSA theory test questions, a full copy of the Highway Code, the Learner Driving programme and certain supplementary notes. All this information is electronically cross-referenced to provide a rich and unique learning environment to assist you in passing your theory and your driving test.

There are three learning programmes that you can follow. Each programme covers all the official questions in a different way. One programme is designed to be used in conjunction with the Highway Code (i.e. just as in this book), one to tie in with the early stages of your practical driving tuition (i.e. the Learner Driving programme) and one to follow the standard theory categories of the DSA.

Whichever programme you choose to follow your progress is carefully monitored and recorded so that you can determine when you are ready for the test.

We have also included a comprehensive mock test environment to help you simulate actual test conditions - thus making sure that nothing is left to chance.

Part 2 - Hazard Perception

Disk 2 contains the official hazard perception practice video clips together with our own video clips to provide a fully working mock test environment. Other video clips are also included to help explain what hazard perception is all about and how the test works.

Hazard perception forms an integral part of the Learner Driving training programme, which is also included on this disk to show you how the theory should be put into practice on a real driving lesson.

The mock test video clips are provided in full and half resolution formats so that lower specification computers can run the video clips smoothly.

Finally, a detailed mock test review process is also included so that you can determine your score and see precisely where the hazards occurred.

System Requirements

Operating System: Windows® 95 / 98 / ME / XP / NT / 2000.
CPU: Pentium 300 or faster.
Free Hard Drive Space: Min install - 30mb Max install - 250mb.
Memory: 64mb (128mb recommended).
Graphics: 800 x 600 + 16bit colour or higher.
CD-Rom Speed: 16 x or faster.
Audio: 16bit SoundBlaster® or 100% compatible

Contents

Introduction
This book covers all the information you need to know to book, take and pass the UK theory test for car drivers first time.

Multiple choice
This is the only book where the official UK theory test questions have been restructured to enable you to easily learn the Highway Code as you prepare for the UK theory test. This will not only help you to learn the Highway Code (essential for a lifetime of safe driving) it will also help you to better remember the correct answers to the theory test questions. This is because most people find it easier to remember things they understand or have studied rather than things they have just tried to memorise.

Most of the other books containing the official questions present the questions in the same order as they were provided by the Driving Standards Agency (i.e. in 14 standard question categories). See the section headed "Cross reference to DSA data bank" for more details. Unfortunately, presenting the questions in this order does not allow you to easily prepare for the theory test using existing books, such as the Highway Code, that contain the theory you need to learn to pass this test and become a safe driver. Consequently, with other books, the reader has to primarily rely upon the use of rote learning (i.e. memorising answers to questions without any form of structured pre-study). This approach is not only tedious it is also very ineffective.

Following a properly structured learning programme, as provided in this book, will enable the learning process to be far more productive and rewarding. With this book you could choose to read a section or two of the Highway Code while travelling to college or work and then undertake the quiz that relates to that study when you get home at night. If you have the CD-rom version of this product (entitled "The Theory Test CD-rom ... made it easy") you could choose to use a computerised quiz, just like the real test, to check what you have learnt that day. By structuring the quizzes to match the study material (i.e. the Highway Code) you can learn the theory in small manageable bits. The alternative, using other books, is to read the whole of the Highway Code and then answer all 893 questions in one big indigestible gulp.

Hazard perception
When the hazard perception test was first introduced into the theory test, in November 2002, the Driving Standards Agency (DSA) allowed professional driving instructors the opportunity to sit this particular test so that they could become familiar with it.

To our surprise on some hazard video clips driving instructors were actually scoring zero out of a possible 5 marks. This was not because the driving instructors were poor at seeing potential hazards, indeed it was just the opposite. On these occasions the driving instructors were clicking the mouse button (this is how you inform the computer that you have seen a hazard) too early, before the potential hazard had become what the DSA term a "developing hazard". Therefore to ensure you get a maximum score on the hazard perception test it helps to fully understand the DSA term "developing hazard" as opposed to "potential hazard" more commonly used by professional driving instructors.

It is also important to understand how the scoring mechanism works. This is why we cover these aspects of the hazard perception test in some detail as part of this book.

Finally, to aid the development of your hazard perception skills we have also included a lesson brief from the highly acclaimed Learner Driving tuition system. This explains what you need to know to start the development of this most important skill.

How to use this book

Once you have read the early sections of this book about the multiple choice test it is time to undertake the 12 quizzes that form the Highway Code quiz programme. However, before you undertake any quiz in this programme you will need to read the appropriate section or sections of the Highway Code as stated at the start of each quiz. Consequently, you will need to buy a copy of the Highway Code or visit www.TheoryTestAdvice.co.uk to view an online copy of this publication. Unfortunately not all the theory necessary to pass this test can be found in the Highway Code. Consequently, we have included a set of supplementary notes for you to read before you embark upon quiz 12. Quiz 12 contains all the official questions not answered by the Highway Code.

To answer any quiz simply take a piece of paper and write down which of the answers to each question you think are correct. If you are unsure of any answer place an asterisk or question mark next to that answer for later review. You can then check your answers by referring to the quiz answers section of this book. Revise the appropriate Highway Code rule, sign, annex or supplementary note of those questions incorrectly answered or that you were unsure about as denoted by the asterisk or question mark. Make a list of the question numbers and then use this list to revise the questions and correct answers just prior to the test. If you have difficulty remembering the answers to any particular question write out the question and correct answer or answers in full. The physical task of doing this will help you to memorise the correct answers to these final questions.

In regards to using this book to help you pass the hazard perception test make sure you study the appropriate sections carefully. This will give you a sound understanding of exactly how the test works, what to expect and what you need to know to start to develop this most important skill.

The only way to become proficient at identifying and dealing with hazards is to take practical lessons from a professional driving instructor. If you want to experience actual test conditions you can purchase the CD-rom version of this product entitled "The Theory Test CD-rom... made it easy" by ringing 01977 691810. However, you will need access to a suitably specified PC for at least a couple of hours to complete this task. See advert opposite Contents page for more details.

Applying for your provisional driving licence

Before you can book a theory test you need to apply for a provisional driving licence from the DVLA in Swansea. You can contact the DVLA direct on 0870 240 0009 to obtain an application form or visit any post office. Certain post offices can also partly process the application for you. Please contact the Post Office customer help line on 08457 223344 for information on participating post office branches.

How to arrange the theory test for your 17th birthday

You can apply for a provisional driving licence when you are sixteen but it will not be valid for learning to drive cars until you are seventeen. However, you can use it to book a theory test up to two months prior to your seventeenth birthday to take place on your birthday or shortly afterwards depending on whether your birthday falls on a normal working day.

Booking the test

You can obtain a theory test application form from your driving instructor, any driving or theory test centre or by telephoning the theory test enquiry line on 0870 0101 372 or 0845 600 6700 in Northern Ireland, between 8am and 6pm Monday to Friday. Welsh speakers can also book on 0870 0100 372. If you are deaf and need a minicom machine telephone 0870 0106 372. If you are able to pay by credit or debit card you can book a theory test appointment direct on the same numbers without the need to complete an application form. You will however, need to quote your driver number from your provisional driving licence. Upon booking you will be given a booking number and sent an appointment letter as confirmation within 8 days.

You can also now book the theory test via the internet on www.driving-tests.co.uk or www.dsa.gov.uk.

Cancelling the test

You are required to give a minimum of three clear working days notice of your decision to cancel or postpone your test, otherwise you will lose your test fee.

Arranging a re-test

If you fail the test you will have to wait a minimum of three clear working days before you can take the test again.

Other languages supported

The test is not only available in English, the following languages are also supported:

Albanian	Hindi	Pushto
Arabic	Kashmiri	Spanish
Bengali	Kurdish	Tamil
Cantonese	Mirpuri	Turkish
Dari	Portuguese	Urdu
Farsi	Polish	Welsh
Gujarati	Punjabi	

Through a headset you will be able to listen to the test being read in any of the above languages. In Northern Ireland other language tests are only available in Cantonese, Bengali and Urdu.

Reading difficulties

The DSA are required to make every effort to ensure that the theory test can be taken by all candidates. However, it is important that you discuss your needs with them when booking the test.

To help candidates with dyslexia or other reading problems a headset can be provided with an English language voice-over. You can also ask for up to double the normal time to complete the test. In such circumstances you will be required to provide a letter from an appropriately qualified individual such as a teacher, psychologist or doctor. If you have any queries please ring the booking number stated earlier and ask for the Special Needs section.

If you cannot read or write in any of the languages provided, you are allowed to bring a translator with you. However, it must be a DSA approved translator.

Hearing difficulties
Both parts of the test can also be delivered in British Sign Language (BSL) by an on-screen signer if you are deaf or have hearing difficulties.

A BSL interpreter or lip operator can be provided if requested at the time of booking.

Foreign licence holders
If your driving licence was issued outside of the EEA (European Economic Area) you will need to check with the Driver Vehicle Licensing Authority (telephone 01792 772151) to determine if your licence is valid in the UK.

At the test centre
You must take one of the following items with you to the test centre.

1. Both parts of your signed photocard driving licence or;

2. your signed driving licence and **photographic identification**.

It would also be helpful if you take your appointment letter or a note of your booking number.

Acceptable forms of **photographic identification** include:
- Your photocard driving licence.
- Your passport, which doesn't have to be a British passport.
- An employers identity or workplace pass bearing your photograph and name or signature or both.
- Trade union card bearing your photograph and signature.
- School Bus Pass bearing the name of the issuing authority and your photograph and signature.
- A signed photograph, together with a suitable statement (as shown on the next page) from a recognised figure of authority. Acceptable certifiers include: Approved Driving Instructor, Member of Parliament, medical practitioner, teacher (qualified), Justice of the Peace, police officer, civil servant (established), bank official, minister of religion, barrister or solicitor.

Certification Statement

I, _____(name of certifier)
certify that this is a true likeness of
_____(name of testee)
who has been known to me for (number)
months/years in my capacity as
_____(occupation)

Signed_____
            (signature of certifier)

Date_____

Daytime phone number

_____

ADI/CBT instructor number

_____

It is extremely important that you arrive in good time at the test centre so that the above documents can be checked. If you arrive after the start time you will not be allowed to sit the test and you will lose your test fee.

The result

At the end of the test you will be given the result for both the multiple choice test and the hazard perception test. To pass the multiple choice test you need to score 30 out of a possible 35 marks. To pass the hazard perception test you need to score 42 out of a possible 75 marks (to be increased in September 2003). If you fail either the multiple choice test or the hazard perception test you will need to take both tests again.

Theory test computer touch screens

Question and answer screen

Question Number

Your Name and Type of test

Time Remaining

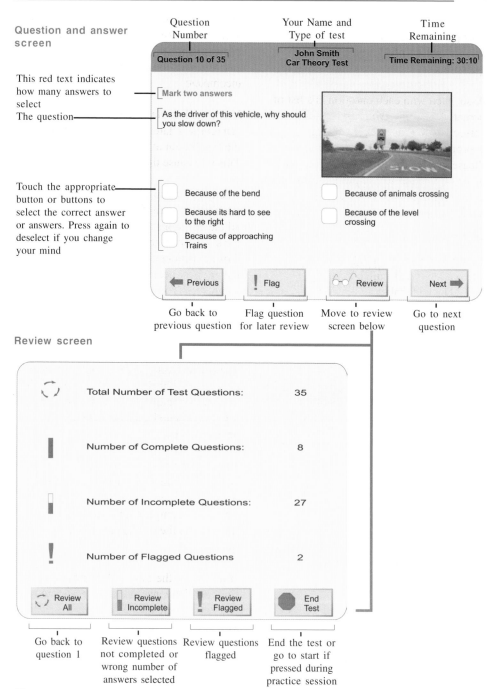

Question 10 of 35

John Smith
Car Theory Test

Time Remaining: 30:10

This red text indicates how many answers to select

The question

Mark two answers

As the driver of this vehicle, why should you slow down?

Touch the appropriate button or buttons to select the correct answer or answers. Press again to deselect if you change your mind

Because of the bend

Because of animals crossing

Because its hard to see to the right

Because of the level crossing

Because of approaching Trains

Previous

Flag

Review

Next

Go back to previous question

Flag question for later review

Move to review screen below

Go to next question

Review screen

Total Number of Test Questions: 35

Number of Complete Questions: 8

Number of Incomplete Questions: 27

Number of Flagged Questions   2

Review All

Review Incomplete

Review Flagged

End Test

Go back to question 1

Review questions not completed or wrong number of answers selected

Review questions flagged

End the test or go to start if pressed during practice session

Introduction

This part of the DSA theory test for car drivers consists of 35 multiple choice questions.

Associated with each question is a list of potential answers. You need to select the correct answer, or answers, by touching the appropriate area of the computer screen. Please see opposite for details. You will be given 40 minutes to complete the test. To pass you need to correctly answer 30 out of the 35 questions (i.e. 86%).

The examination process

Before you start the actual test a short video tutorial will explain how the test should be undertaken. You will be given the opportunity to complete some practice questions to make sure you are familiar with the computer screens.

As you can see from the layout of the theory test computer screens opposite, you move from one question to the next by touching the arrowed buttons at the bottom.

To select any particular answer press the button on the screen next to the answer you wish to select. The answer will then be highlighted with a blue background. To unselect an answer simply touch the answer button on the screen again. This will cause the highlighted blue background to disappear.

The red text in the top left hand corner will tell you how many answers to mark (i.e. to select). This text will flash if you have not selected sufficient answers and try to move

onto another screen. If you press again it will let you move on even if you still haven't supplied sufficient answers. In this case the question will be recorded as incomplete.

If you wish to flag a question so that you can review it later you will need to press the flag button at the bottom of the screen. This will cause the flag button to turn red.

At any point you can call up the review screen. This screen enables you to check all the questions and your answers from the start. Alternatively you can just review those questions flagged or those questions incomplete (i.e. not fully answered or not attempted). You will also need to press the review button so that you can end the test. To end the test you press the end test button on the review screen.

The test will automatically end if you run out of time. The time you have left to finish answering the questions is shown at the top right hand side of the question and answer screen.

Hints and tips

Before you press on the end test button in the review screen make sure that the number of complete questions equals 35, the same as the total number of test questions.

If this is not the case review those questions not fully answered or not attempted (i.e. incomplete questions), and any that you have flagged. Incomplete questions require you to select one or more answers until you have marked the required number

as indicated by the red text in the top left
hand corner of the question and answer
screen.

Even if you have completed all the questions, and provided you have the time, it is
worth the effort of reviewing all your
answers again before pressing the end test
button.

Once you have completed the test you will
be given the option of a 3 minute break
before you move on to the next part of the
test, hazard perception.

Analysing the results

At the end of the theory test you will be
given your result for this part of the test
and a list of those DSA categories where
you answered a question incorrectly.
Unfortunately, the DSA will not tell you
which questions were wrongly answered
only the category they relate to. To help
you find the questions in this book that
relate to any particular DSA category we
have provided a cross reference to the DSA
data bank of questions in the same order as
they appear in the DSA's official theory test
book. This cross reference will help you
should you fail an attempt at the multiple
choice test and wish to revise those
questions specific to any one of the 14 DSA
categories.

About the hazard perception test

Introduction

This part of the theory test requires you to view 14 hazard video clips on the computer screen of approximately one minute each. You are required to watch these clips as if you were the driver. There will be 15 hazards to find - at least one on each clip. However, one clip will have 2 hazards. The hazard clips will not contain any sound - just like the old silent movies.

You click the mouse button whenever you think you can see a hazard developing. The speed at which you click the mouse button as a hazard develops will determine your score for that particular hazard clip. You can score between 0 and 5 on each hazard. Therefore the maximum you can score is 75 (i.e. 15 hazards x 5). To pass you need a score of 42 (to be increased in September 2003).

The examination process

The hazard perception part of the theory test will start with a short video tutorial played on the computer screen that will explain how the hazard perception test works and what you are required to do. At the end of this clip you have the option to go onto the test or play the tutorial again.

Each hazard clip will start with a freeze frame of the start of the video sequence and a count down from 10 will commence. At the end of the count down the clip will start to play and you will be required to click the mouse button each time you see a developing hazard.

To let you know that the program has registered your click a red flag will appear on a grey band across the bottom of the screen - one flag for each click you make in any particular clip. At the end of the clip all the flags will be removed before you start the next clip.

Although each clip contains several potential hazards only the one that materialises into a real hazard and involves other road users is marked . This is known as a "developing hazard". Therefore you will only receive a score if you spot a hazard before it fully materialises and is brought about by the action of another road user. You will know if the hazard materialises because the driver will have to take evasive action (e.g. slow down, stop or swerve out of the way).

The score you obtain will be dependant upon how quickly you spot the developing hazard. The time from when the developing hazard could be potentially seen on the screen to when the vehicle arrives at the hazard is the time frame or window used to determine your score.

Time

Potential Hazard

5 Points   4 Points   3 Points   2 Points   1 Points

Actual Hazard

Developing hazard window

This window of time is divided into 5 equal segments. If you click the mouse while in the first segment (i.e. just as the developing hazard appears) you will obtain the maximum score of 5 points. If you click in the second segment of this window of time you will score 4 points, then 3, then 2 and then in the last segment just 1. This is accurate to one twenty fifth of a second.

If you click several times during this window of time the computer will always take your highest score and record that for that particular clip. If you don't click the mouse button in this window of time you will score nothing in respect to that hazard.

If you try to cheat the system by clicking the button repeatedly throughout the video clip the computer program will pick this up. It does this by analysing the number of clicks over the clip as a whole and the pattern of clicks. Within the scoring window no such checks are made and if you click several times in this window only the first click will be used to determine your score, as stated earlier (i.e. the highest scoring click).

There is a certain maximum number of permitted clicks for any clip. However, this is far higher than the potential hazards anybody could reasonably perceive. If the computer program determines that you may be cheating a message window will appear at the end of the clip letting you know that an irregular clicking activity was detected and that as a result the score for that clip will be zero.

When the clip ends the screen will turn black for a few seconds before the freeze frame for the next video clip appears and the count down commences again, warning you to get ready. This pattern is repeated until all 14 video clips have been shown.

At the end of the hazard perception part of the theory test you will be given the option to complete a customer care survey if you so wish.

You will then be directed to leave the room and collect your score for the two parts of the exam. The maximum score that can be obtained for the hazard perception part of the theory test is 75 (i.e. 15x5). To pass the hazard perception part of the car, moped and motorcycle theory test you must obtain a score of 42. This pass mark may be increased in September 2003. To pass the theory test you must pass both parts. If you fail either part you are required to take both parts of the test again.

Hints and tips

When watching the video clips do not be frightened to click the mouse button whenever you see a potential hazard involving another road user (i.e. anything that you think may cause the driver to change speed, position or direction). Watch the hazard and if it continues to materialise continue to click the mouse button. This will ensure that you click within the scoring window.

Some of these potential hazards will not materialise and therefore you will not receive a score for spotting them. For example, if the cyclist shown in the developing hazard sequence on the previous page stopped at the end of the side road (i.e. at the 4 point stage) the hazard would not have materialised (also see page 25 official hazard clip 3). In the actual clip the cyclist was travelling too fast to stop. This was the real clue to what was going to happen next.

In a few instances it is difficult to determine when a potential hazard becomes a developing hazard and therefore when the scoring window should start. This is why it is safer to click a few times as you see a hazard develop to make sure you don't click too early and miss the opening of this window.

In this second example also supplied by the DSA you will notice a very young child riding a bike on the pavement (also see page 24 official hazard clip 2). This alone may be classified as a potential hazard, particularly as the child is unsupervised.

However, the scoring window on this clip doesn't open until the child starts to turn towards the road to cross it as shown below and highlighted by the red circle. This is the point at which the potential hazard becomes a developing hazard and the scoring window opens.

Therefore if you had only clicked your mouse button once as you saw the child riding her bike along the pavement you would have scored zero. Therefore, remember to click the button a couple of times as the hazard develops to avoid this problem.

The main type of hazards that you will need to look for in this test are:
i) pedestrians or cyclists crossing the road;
ii) vehicles emerging from side roads, parking places or driveways;
iii) large vehicles moving over to your side of the road;
iv) meeting oncoming vehicles on narrow roads or where other obstructions or slow moving vehicles make the road narrow and finally;
v) where animals may wander onto the road.

To further help you prepare for this part of the test we have included:

i) a section that contains the hazard perception and defensive driving lesson brief taken from the Learner Driving programme of driving tuition (see page opposite) and;

ii) a section that shows you the scoring windows of each of the eight official hazard perception practice video clips supplied by the Driving Standards Agency (DSA).

Hazard perception and defensive driving lesson brief

Introduction

In this section we have included the lesson brief on hazard perception and defensive driving taken from the Learner Driving programme of driving tuition. This represents lesson 11 in the programme. If you want to read all the lesson briefs in the Learner Driving programme please visit our website at www.TheoryTestAdvice.co.uk under the section driving lessons.

Lesson brief - introduction

During this lesson you will learn how to deal with much busier traffic situations. To do this effectively you will need to further develop your hazard perception skills (i.e. your ability to recognise potential hazards) and your defensive driving skills (i.e. your ability to deal with them).

You will recall from lesson 6 that a hazard may be defined as anything that may require you to change speed, position or direction of your vehicle. Basically hazards can be caused by static road features (e.g. junctions, bends, humps, dips, passing places, traffic lights, bridges, crossings, road works, parked vehicles, wet leaves, spilt oil, surface water etc) or by the actions of other road users or a combination of the two.

Although static road features can present a hazard the routine for dealing with them and the type of hazard they present is covered elsewhere in the Learner Driving programme. In this part of the programme we will be concentrating on those hazards that develop through the actions of other road users and those circumstances that can contribute to their hazardous behaviour.

Hazard Perception; a bit of detection work!

Perception in driving terms can be defined as: 'The art of being able to pick out the important details from all the information being supplied by your sensors.' A perceptive driver must look for clues and build up a mental picture of what they think may happen next.

While hazard perception skills can only truly be acquired through experience (preferably under the guidance of an appropriately qualified professional driving instructor) you can speed up the learning process by having a better understanding of the factors that an expert driver considers when building up this mental picture of what's likely to happen next. These are the main factors that an expert driver would consider:

Road signs

Road signs can provide you with a clear warning of what lies ahead. It is essential that you train yourself to take note of all road signs and act accordingly.

Your location

Are you in a busy town centre or on a country road? It would be unlikely that you would meet a flock of sheep in the High Street, but there may be one just around the next corner on a country road. Whatever your location you must always consider the type of hazard that you may expect to meet there, and be driving at such a speed that you can stop safely, if necessary.

The time of day

The time of day can give you a lot of information about what to expect on the road. If you see a warning sign for cattle, or mud on the road you should be especially vigilant at dawn or dusk because cows are often taken for milking at these times and may well be on the road ahead ... perhaps around the next bend.

Although children can be present in the road at any time, they are out in force just before and after school. Therefore, you should be keeping a special look out for children during the morning rush hour and mid-afternoon periods.

Other road users

It may seem fairly obvious that you should look out for other road users, but remember, you are not just looking for them, you are looking for clues about what they will do next?

Pedestrians: The Highway Code explains that those pedestrians most at risk on the road are over 60 or less than 15. Old people do not judge speed and distance very well and their reactions can be slow. Have they seen you? Can they hear you? Look for clues. Are they carrying a white stick? Are they looking your way? And so on.

Children have little time to consider road safety; they are more interested in the game that they are playing or the ice cream van that they are running after. Look for clues. Are they alone? If one child runs or cycles into the road there will often be at least one more following; footballs are followed by children; cycles, seemingly abandoned at the side of the road, will mean that children are not far away.

All pedestrians, not just the young and old, are at risk on the road. If there are pedestrians about, make sure that you know what they are going to do before they do it.

Animals: are frightened by noise and vehicles. Therefore, drive slowly, don't sound your horn or rev up the engine and keep you distance. Watch their behaviour carefully, particularly if it is a horse being ridden by a child.

Cyclists: A High Court judge once ruled that a cyclist is entitled to wobble. Drivers should have more control over their vehicles than cyclists who are dependent upon physical strength and effort to pilot their machines.

Always leave plenty of room when passing cyclists, look out for clues about their next move. For example, a cyclist who looks around over his or her right shoulder may be about to turn right; a puddle in the road will cause a cyclist to move out. Cyclists are not easy to see and they can easily get lost in the blind spots around your vehicle such as those caused by your windscreen and door pillars. Particularly watch out for them in slow moving traffic in built up areas – they may overtake you on either side when you least expect.

Motorcyclists: Like cyclists motorcyclists are not easy to see particularly at dusk and at night. Like cyclists they may also take up unusual road positions to avoid holes and bumps in the road surface. It is very easy to miss an approaching motorcyclist when emerging at junctions – so remember think once, think twice, think bike!

Drivers: If you are unsure about what a driver is going to do next, leave plenty of space between you and them. A sporty looking "custom-car" may be driven by someone more interested in "posing" than driving.

Look out for the actions of drivers: a driver who has just stopped may open his door without checking to see if it is safe; a driver who seems to be dithering about may be a stranger to the area and could, therefore, make a last minute turn without a signal when he or she sees the road they are looking for.

Large vehicles: Buses and large vehicles need more room and may take up unusual road positions to turn round corners at junctions etc. Hold back and give them plenty of room.

Inconsistent behaviour
Inconsistent behaviour is often a very good clue to what might happen next. Just because a bus is signalling left prior to the side road that you intend to emerge from doesn't mean that you should go on the assumption that the bus is turning left? Look to see if all the actions of the driver are consistent with the signal. Is the vehicle slowing down as you would expect to complete the proposed turn? Is the position

of the vehicle consistent with the proposed manoeuvre? Is the driver looking in the direction they intend to turn? Could the driver be signalling left for any other reason? In this example the bus driver may be signalling left to pull up at a bus stop just after the side road. Make sure you look at all the evidence before you finally decide.

Train your mind to recognise inconsistency – that's not quite right – why's that?

What other drivers cannot see
Consider what you can see that other drivers cannot see. This may play an important part in determining what may happen next. Consider whether you can see something or someone that they cannot see that may cause them to alter their course or abort the manoeuvre at the last minute. Also consider whether other drivers need to see you and if so determine what you can do to make your presence know to them.

The weather and visibility
Bright sunlight, fog, rain and snow can severely affect visibility therefore remember to slow down and give yourself more space.

At dusk and at night the driver loses the ability to see any detail and dark objects easily merge into the background. Consider not only how this may affect your judge-ment but also how these conditions may affect other drivers. Is the other driver being blinded by bright sunlight or if at night by headlights on full beam? Are the windows of other vehicles misty - can the driver see you? Will the high-sided vehicle, in high wind, remain stable when it crosses a gap in the hedge or buildings that might line the side of the road?

Also remember the effects of water, ice and snow on the road surface – are the other drivers driving too fast for the weather conditions – are you driving too fast for these conditions?

Defensive driving
Driving defensively is all about giving yourself time to react and keeping your options open. Even someone with lightening fast reactions needs time to react. The laws of physics simply prevent a car from stopping dead. Even if you are Superman or Superwoman, with

supernatural reactions, you couldn't stop a car within fewer car lengths than those shown below:

this effectively you need to:

· **Look well ahead and perceive potential problems early.**

· **Apply your hazard drill in good time.**

· **Give yourself plenty of space.**

Look well ahead and perceive potential problems early
See and be seen. Take up safe road positions that allow you to see and be seen. Be attentive; focus on the driving task - don't let your mind wander.

Keep your eyes moving and scan the road well ahead. Avoid staring at any single point ahead or to the side. Concentrate on

Instant reactions: No thinking time needed

30 mph
40 mph
50 mph
70 mph

Consequently, anything or anybody who is within the distances shown above of the front of your car will be hit! You could call this area to the front of your car the impact zone or if you are travelling at 40 MPH or more the killing zone as anyone hit at these speeds is unlikely to survive. This clearly demonstrates the importance of anticipating what might happen and acting upon that rather than waiting until it happens. To do

the available space (i.e. the gaps), not the obstructions.

With experience and guidance from your instructor you will begin to recognise what feedback from your sensors are important and what is not. Ignore the superficial information you can see. For example don't concentrate on identifying individual drivers or pedestrians or the make, model or the colours of vehicles. Instead concentrate on the position, speed and potential course of other vehicles and/or pedestrians both to the front, rear and sides of your vehicle.

Look as far down the road as you can see for any potential hazards whether they are static road features or situations being caused by other road users. A gap in the tree line ahead may mean that there is a side road at that point or an upside down triangle sign in the distance may warn you that you are approaching a T Junction and so on.

Initially you may perceive risks that aren't really there or indeed ignore risks that are. With experience you will begin to develop your own judgement in this regard.

Apply the hazard drill in good time

The hazard drill that we recommend and use is based on a simplified version of the police system of vehicle control. The manoeuvre part of the Mirror-Signal-Manoeuvre routine (MSM) is split into Position-Speed-Gear. See the diagram below.

Hazard drill (MSPSG)

Each time you are presented with a potential or actual hazard on the road (i.e. anything that may require you to have to change speed, position or direction) you will go through the following hazard drill one or more times. While each step of the drill needs to be considered in the order shown it need not necessarily be acted upon. Observations to the front, rear and sides are carried out at the start and as necessary throughout the application of the drill.

Mirrors: Use your interior mirror and side mirror(s) early. Glance into your right and left blind spots as appropriate. Because this forms part of your observations this part of the drill may be repeated at any point throughout the drill as required.

Signal: Give signals in good time. Use signals to help or warn other road users. Be careful not to give misleading signals.

Position: Determine the best position/course to negotiate the hazard. Think before you change position; be careful not to mislead others.

Speed: Adjust your speed so that you can negotiate the hazard ahead and stop within the distance you can see to be clear.

Gear: Select the gear to match your speed and the power you need. Make sure that the gear is selected before the hazard is negotiated.

Take observations as necessary throughout the drill

MIRRORS → SIGNAL → POSITION → SPEED → GEAR
(Must)   (Surely)   (Prevent)   (Some)   (Grief)

As soon as you perceive a potential danger begin to employ this hazard drill and determine where you can go or how you can stop if the danger materialises. Remember you need to consider what's behind as well as what is in front when considering your options.

Give yourself plenty of space

You need to give yourself the time to recognise a potential problem and apply the hazard drill. We refer to this as **"driving in space"**.

Driving in space is all about maintaining a buffer of 'safety space' or if you like a safety bubble all around you at all times. The higher your speed (or greater your stopping distance) the bigger the bubble needs to be.

· Space to the front

Always allow yourself enough room to stop. On narrow country roads with a limited view, this may be as much as twice your overall stopping distance (to leave room for the idiot coming the other way!).

· Space to the sides

Make sure that you leave enough room for pedestrians, cyclists, motorcyclists and other vehicles. If you are unsure whether or not you will fit through a gap, you won't! Give parked cars and pedestrians at the side of the road plenty of clearance. Remember pedestrians are far more vulnerable then vehicles. Allow for car doors opening or children appearing from between parked cars or pedestrians wandering onto the road particularly in crowded streets or joggers on country roads moving out to avoid puddles or mud on the road side. Position your car accordingly and reduce speed as the space to your sides is reduced.

· Space to the rear

If other vehicles follow too close slow down and let them pass. Remember that it's your neck that will suffer if someone hits your car from the back! The less space you have at the back the more you need at the front.

Start of score 5 segment

Start of score 2 segment

Start of score 4 segment

Start of score 1 segment

Start of score 3 segment

Back to score zero

Start of score 5 segment

Start of score 2 segment

Start of score 4 segment

Start of score 1 segment

Start of score 3 segment

Back to score zero

Official hazard perception practice clip 3

Start of score 5 segment

Start of score 2 segment

Start of score 4 segment

Start of score 1 segment

Start of score 3 segment

Back to score zero

Start of score 5 segment

Start of score 2 segment

Start of score 4 segment

Start of score 1 segment

Start of score 3 segment

Back to score zero

Start of score 5 segment

Start of score 2 segment

Start of score 4 segment

Start of score 1 segment

Start of score 3 segment

Back to score zero

Start of score 5 segment

Start of score 4 segment

Start of score 3 segment

Start of score 2 segment

Start of score 1 segment

Back to score zero

Official hazard perception practice clip 7

Start of score 5 segment

Start of score 2 segment

Start of score 4 segment

Start of score 1 segment

Start of score 3 segment

Back to score zero

Start of score 5 segment

Start of score 2 segment

Start of score 4 segment

Start of score 1 segment

Start of score 3 segment

Back to score zero

Introduction

Unfortunately about 12% of the theory test questions cannot be answered by the Highway Code. Consequently, we have grouped these questions together and put them into quiz 12. Therefore before you undertake quiz 12 you will need to read the following supplementary notes. Please note a more comprehensive version of these notes can be found on the website www.TheoryTestAdvice.co.uk under the heading Driving Lessons and Highway Code. However, the condensed version that follows is still sufficient to answer all the questions in the theory test that do not relate to the Highway Code.

1. Motor Insurance

It is a legal requirement that before you drive a vehicle on public roads you have the proper insurance cover. Indeed to obtain a vehicle excise licence (i.e. a tax disc) it is necessary for you to have insurance cover. There are three main types. These are:

- Third Party Insurance
  This is the legal minimum cover and is also the cheapest. It covers anyone who you might injure or whose property you might damage. It does not cover your own property or injury to yourself.
- Third Party, Fire and Theft
  This offers the same benefits as third party insurance but also covers your own vehicle should it be damaged by fire or stolen.
- Fully Comprehensive
  This is the best and the most expensive. As well as the benefits of the two previous types it also covers damage to your own vehicle and injury to yourself.

The cost of insurance (i.e. the premium paid) varies from company to company and also depends on certain factors. These include:

- Age of driver (e.g. people in the age group 17 25 years are the most likely to have an accident, therefore the younger the driver the more expensive the insurance).
- Make of vehicle.
- Size of engine.

- Number of years driving experience.
- Full or provisional licence holder.
- Court convictions, if any.
- Where you live.
- Where the vehicle is to be kept and if it has an alarm.
- Intended use of vehicle.
- No Claims Bonus (a discount given to drivers off their insurance premium for each year they do not make a claim).
- Amount of excess (the amount you are required to pay towards each claim the higher the excess the lower the premium).
- Completion of Pass Plus Scheme (a scheme to give new drivers more experience by taking further training with an Approved Driving Instructor after passing their test). Everyone who takes and passes the course will get reduced premiums with certain insurance companies.

A Cover Note is a document issued by an Insurance Company on receipt of a deposit, or full premium which has been paid for third party only, third party, fire and theft, or comprehensive insurance cover for your vehicle for the risks stated. This document is usually issued for a limited period of time, which is normally one calendar month from the date of issue. The Cover Note is a temporary substitute which is issued until such times as a proper insurance certificate, can by provided by the Insurance Company concerned.

2. The Environment

The car is no longer a luxury. It has now become an essential part of modern life. As more and more cars are using our roads they are unfortunately having a detrimental effect on the environment.

As fuel is burned in the engine it produces waste gases which are toxic and harmful. These pollutants are released into the air causing damage to plant life and human health problems such as asthma. Buildings are now showing the effects of these pollutants as stone and brickwork start to deteriorate.

The more cars that are being used means that we need to make more roads or widen the existing ones. This changes the landscape and disrupts wildlife. More fuel is also being used which depletes our natural resources, pollutes the air and adds to global warming.

All modern vehicles with a petrol engine are now fitted with a catalytic converter. Catalytic Converters reduce the harmful gases given out by the engine, such as exhaust emissions, their function is to act like a filter, removing some of the toxic waste normally given out, into the air. The MOT test now includes a strict emissions test to ensure that car engines are properly tuned so that pollution is reduced.

The responsibility for looking after the environment cannot rest solely on the shoulders of the motor vehicle manufacturers. Drivers themselves can do a lot to reduce the effects of pollution, for example:

- Share a vehicle with someone who makes the same journey.
- Walk or cycle instead of using the car.
- Avoid using the car for very short journeys particularly when the engine is cold.
- Use public transport.
- Make sure your car is properly serviced and the engine is correctly tuned.
- Inflate your tyres to the correct pressure. Under inflated tyres increase fuel consumption.
- Avoid rapid acceleration or harsh braking because this leads to increased fuel consumption.
- Slow down as the faster you go the more fuel you will use. At 70mph a vehicle will use up to 30% more fuel than at 50mph.
- Do not carry unnecessary weight in your car.
- Remove your roof rack when not in use.
- Have your vehicle's engine converted to unleaded fuel.
- Plan well ahead when driving so as to avoid braking hard.
- Do not over rev the engine in the lower gears.

If you service your own car do not dispose of the old engine oil by pouring it down the drain as it is harmful to the environment, illegal and could result in prosecution. Also be careful about the way you dispose of the car battery as this also poses a potential hazard to the environment. In both cases take them to a local authority refuse site or garage who will have facilities to dispose of them safely. Remember, this is our world and we must do everything we can to protect it.

If in a city use trams where available. They are environmentally friendly because they reduce noise pollution, use electricity and reduce town traffic.

3. Tyres

It is vitally important that the tyres on your car are in good condition and inflated to the correct pressure. They are your only contact with the road and will not grip safely if they are in bad condition. Check the condition of your tyres regularly and replace them if necessary. The walls of the tyres should be free from cuts and bulges.

The tread depth should be a minimum of 1.6mm across the central three quarters of the breadth of the tyre and around the entire circumference. This is the minimum legal requirement.

If the tyres are worn unevenly this could be due to the wheels not being aligned or balanced correctly. Alternatively it may be a fault with the suspension or braking systems. Get it checked and put right. If the wheels are not balanced correctly this can cause a vibration on the steering wheel as you drive.

Tyre pressures should be checked weekly and before any long journey, particularly one which will include motorway driving. Always try to check pressures when the tyres are cold so as to get a more accurate reading. Recommended tyre pressures for each vehicle can be found in the owner's handbook.

Tyres can be inflated to a higher pressure (but never more than the recommended maximum) when carrying a heavy load or driving at speed for long distances. Under-inflated tyres can reduce stability, make steering heavy, affect breaking efficiency and cause the car to use more fuel. It is an offence to drive a car with an incorrectly inflated tyre.

4. Fuel
Leaded petrol is becoming increasingly unpopular because of its high lead content and bad effect on the environment. Used mainly in older cars, it is gradually being phased out.

5. Power Steering
Power steering is becoming increasingly common in modern cars. A motor assists the driver when he turns the steering wheel, making it easier to steer as the driver does not need as much strength to turn the wheel. The steering on a car fitted with power steering seems lighter than that on a car fitted with conventional steering.

Because of this you need to be particularly careful not to steer while the vehicle is stationary as this may cause damage to the tyres and the steering mechanism.

6. Oil and electrics
Oil is a vital component needed to lubricate the engine of your car. Check the oil level weekly and before any long journey. Top up as required with the correct grade of oil.

How to check the oil level
- Oil should be checked when the engine is cold.
- Park your car on level ground.
- Raise bonnet and locate the dipstick on the engine block.
- Take the dipstick out and wipe clean with a dry-cloth.
- Note the markings on the dipstick which indicate the lowest and highest levels.
- Push the dipstick fully back into the engine block.
- Take the dipstick out and see where the oil level has reached.

- If oil is below the minimum then top up as required, being careful not to overfill as this will cause excessive pressure that could damage the engine seals and gaskets and cause oil leaks. It can also result in the vehicle's exhaust becoming very smoky. If oil is above the minimum then no oil is required.

How to check your battery fluid levels
The distilled water in your battery cells may occasionally need to be topped up. You do this by filling each cell until the distilled water is just above the cell plate.

7. Brakes
You can check the brake fluid level regularly and keep it topped up by following the instructions in the owner's handbook.

Excessive use of the foot brake, particularly when travelling down a long steep downhill gradient, will normally cause the brakes to overheat and they are liable to become less effective. This is known as "Brake Fade" which is more likely to happen on cars fitted with drum brakes, but it can still apply to those fitted with disc brakes as well. To assist with the control of the car and avoid brake fade, it is advisable to make use of an appropriate lower gear in accordance with the steepness of gradient.

8. Cooling System
The level of water/coolant mix must not be allowed to drop below the minimum level marked on the bottle. Instructions on how to refill and keep it topped up can be found in the owner's handbook.

9. Distractions
When driving it is important that your attention is concentrated on the task of driving and that there are no unnecessary distractions.

Do not hang anything from the rear view mirror as it will restrict your view as well as distract your attention.

Playing loud music will prevent you from hearing anything else, particularly the sirens of emergency vehicles. You can gain a lot of information about your surroundings by listening as well as looking.

Do not drive if you are angry or upset as this will seriously affect your concentration. If you are still feeling angry after an argument, you should always give yourself time to calm down, before attempting to set out on any journey.

10. Mirrors

There are three main mirrors fitted to your car: an interior mirror and two exterior mirrors. The surface of the exterior mirrors is usually convex which gives a wider field of vision but makes vehicles appear to be further away than they actually are. The surface of the interior mirror is flat, making it easier to judge the speed, distance and position of following vehicles than when looking in the exterior mirrors.

If you are dazzled by the lights of following vehicles when driving at night set your interior mirror to 'antidazzle'. Just behind the lower edge of the mirror is a small lever pull this forward and you will still be able to see the lights of the vehicles behind but the dazzle will be greatly reduced. Always remember to reset the mirror by pushing the lever towards the windscreen.

11. Dashboard

There are several warning lights which come on to warn the driver of any problems or to give information about the functions selected. Details of all the warning lights on your car can be found

in the owner's handbook. Make sure you know what these lights mean. Three of the most important lights are described below:

Brake Warning Light "!"

If this light with an exclamation mark in a circle comes on when you are driving it could indicate that there is a fault within the braking system. This could be dangerous and so you should stop as soon as you can, trying not to rely on the brakes too much, and get the braking system checked by a qualified mechanic. This light may also come on when the handbrake is applied so make sure you release the handbrake fully and the light goes out.

Parking Brake Light "P"

Some cars have this light with the letter "P" in a circle. This light comes on when the handbrake is applied. If the hand-brake is not released properly the light will stay on. Also see above.

Headlight/Fog light indicator lights "=D"

This light with a side view of a headlight with a series of vertical lines in front indicates that your lights are on full beam as opposed to dipped beam.

12. Stopping in an Emergency

If you need to stop in an emergency quick reactions can save vital seconds and even a life. React as soon as you can, while keeping control of the car by retaining both hands on the steering wheel.

The quicker you apply the foot brake the sooner the car will stop. Be careful though. If you press the brake too hard or 'slam' the brakes on your car is likely to skid. Some modern cars are fitted with an antilocking brake system (ABS) which senses when the wheels are about to lock and very quickly releases the braking pressure such that the wheels are allowed to turn very slowly spreading the frictional force over more of the tyre. This allows optimum braking to be achieved on a normal road surface while allowing the driver to steer the car at the same time. ABS is slightly less effective on icy, wet or loose surfaces and the brakes are only as good as the tyre grip on the road.

13. First Aid

It may happen that one day you come across the scene of, or are involved in, an accident so it may be helpful to be familiar with a few basic first aid procedures. Firstly there is the ABC procedure for dealing with unconscious accident victims. Please refer to the Highway Code Annex 7 first aid on the road, pages 92-93. The B part of the procedure stands for breathing. Although the Highway Code explains how to give mouth to mouth resuscitation it does not explain the need to blow particularly **gently** when dealing with a young child.

Back Injury

Any casualty you suspect has a back or neck injury should not be moved unless they are in danger. Movement could add to the injury. Do not remove the safety helmet of an injured motorcyclist unless it is absolutely essential as serious injury could result.

Burns

If any casualty is suffering from burns, no matter how severe, it is possible that they could go into immediate nervous shock. This will cause them to go pale, confused, anxious, frightened or they may even faint.

Douse the burns with a cold, clean, non-toxic liquid unless they are very severe, in which case the burn should be lightly covered with a clean cloth and professional medical attention sought immediately. Never try to remove anything which is stuck to the burn. Leave that to the experts.

14. Hills

When going uphill it is more difficult to maintain or increase speed as the engine has to work harder to make the car go faster. You may find you will need to change to a lower gear to give you more power. Ideally you should change down before you start to climb the hill.

The brakes will slow the car down quicker when going uphill. Remember to apply the handbrake once you have stopped on an uphill gradient otherwise the car will roll back.

When going downhill the engine is helped along by the weight of the car (i.e. gravity) and so it will travel faster, making it more difficult to slow down, as the brakes have less effect. Select a lower gear before you start to go down a hill. Using a lower gear in this manner to reduce the speed of the car is known as engine braking.

15. Fuel Spillage

Fuel is a precious commodity and all precautions to avoid wasting it should be taken. If you suspect that the fuel tank of your vehicle is leaking have it checked and, if necessary, replaced. Your leaking fuel tank may result in a fire or an explosion. While leaking diesel might not ignite it will make the road surface extremely slippery. When refuelling make sure you do not overfill the tank and ensure that the filler cap is securely fastened.

16. Manoeuvring

You can legally remove your seat belt when performing any manoeuvre that includes reversing. This allows you greater freedom to move around and turn your head for better observation. Always check all around before you start to reverse. If you are not sure whether or not it is clear behind your vehicle, get out and have a look. If you cannot see clearly as you reverse get someone to guide you.

There are many dangers as you reverse, mainly from approaching traffic and pedestrians. Keep your speed down and give yourself time to take good observations. Before you steer check for other road users as the front of your vehicle may swing out into the path of another vehicle.

17. Vehicle Loading

As a driver it is your responsibility to ensure that your vehicle is loaded properly and safely. If you have to carry a load it must be fastened securely and not stick out dangerously. A heavy load on a roof rack will reduce the stability of your vehicle and make it more difficult to handle.

18. Signs and Markings

The majority of road signs and road markings are explained in The Highway Code. However there are a few less common ones which are not included. Some of these are explained below.

This sign with a "P" over a car on a raised verge on a blue background means that you may legally park your car fully on the verge or footpath.

 This arrow sign with a "P +" and a silhouette of a bus on a blue background is becoming more common. It indicates an area where a Park and Ride system is in operation. You can park your car in an out-of-town car park and a bus service is provided to take you into the town. This system is successful in keeping traffic out of busy town centres.

You will find this sign with an "R" on a green background at intervals alongside the road, indicating that you are travelling on the Ring Road.

 On the approach to a concealed railway crossing you might see countdown markings denoting the distance to the stop line. Red diagonal strips on a white background. Each red strip represents one third of the distance to the level crossing, i.e. 150 yards, 100 yards, 50 yards or similarly 90 yards, 60 yards, 30 yards.

Drivers sometimes ignore "SCHOOL KEEP CLEAR" road makings that are used to mark where school children cross the road. The markings are there to inform drivers not to wait or park in this area. To do so would cause danger by potentially blocking the view of children

crossing the road or drivers driving up or down the road.

Yellow lines are sometimes painted across the road surface on the approach to a hazard, such as a roundabout. Their function is to make the driver aware of his speed and direct them to slow down.

Some road markings, such as the white lines between the motorway carriageway and the hard shoulder, have raised areas at regular intervals which make a noise as you drive over them. These rumble devices are there to alert the driver to a hazard, in this case the edge of the carriageway, or to encourage the driver to slow down as would be the case if the yellow lines illustrated above were slightly raised. Red raised lines may be used in place of the yellow lines for exactly the same purpose.

To separate traffic flowing in opposite directions, particularly on bends, you may see an area in the middle of the road painted red enclosed with broken or unbroken white lines with white diagonal strips. This area is designed to discourage drivers from moving too close to the centre of the road and therefore present a hazard to oncoming vehicles that may do the same.

When driving through a tunnel make sure you look out for variable message signs. These signs will provide warnings and orders as necessary.

 This sign with a silhouette of a man running towards an open door on a green background is found in tunnels, indicating the Emergency Exit For Pedestrians.

19. Lane Discipline

If you find that you are in the wrong lane do not move across immediately. Carry on in that lane until you can change lanes safely or, if it is not possible to change lanes, continue in your lane and find another way back to your route.

The same applies to a one-way street. If you find yourself travelling down a one-way street but you need to go in the opposite direction, you must not turn round. Continue to the end of the road and then find an alternative route to your destination.

20. Towing

When towing a caravan or trailer there are a few basic principles you need to follow. Never exceed the manufacturer's recommended maximum weight that can be towed by your car or the maximum nose weight that can be applied to the tow ball (details can be found in owner's handbook). It is usually safest for the loaded weight of the trailer not to exceed 85% of the kerbside (empty) weight of the towing vehicle. Passengers must never be allowed to travel in a caravan when it is being towed. Fit exterior mirrors with extending arms so you can see clearly along both sides of the trailer. Fit a stabiliser to the tow bar to help reduce the effects of cross winds.

Before starting on a journey ensure that the trailer is correctly hitched and that the breakaway cable is properly connected. Should the trailer and the towing vehicle become separated this will break and apply the brakes to the trailer.

21. Automatic Transmission

A car fitted with automatic transmission will change gear automatically. Sometimes the driver may need quick acceleration, for example to overtake. This can be achieved by pressing the accelerator pedal all the way to the floor, causing a quick change to a lower gear, so speed can be increased quickly. This technique is known as 'kick down'.

22. Four Wheel Drive

Most cars are two wheel drive which means that either the front or rear wheels are driven by the engine, the other two are either pushed or pulled along. However some vehicles are fitted with four wheel drive which means that all four wheels are driven by the engine. One of the main benefits of this system is that road holding is improved.

23. Emergency Vehicles

When driving along always be on the look out for emergency vehicles. You can recognise them by their flashing blue lights and loud sirens. They include police, fire brigade, ambulance, coastguard, blood transfusion service, bomb disposal and mountain rescue vehicles. If you see a vehicle with a green flashing light treat it just the same as this is a doctor on an emergency call out.

24. Junctions and bends

Special care must be taken when emerging from a junction (going from the side road into the main road).

Make good, early observations as you approach. This will help you to decide if you can see clearly enough to determine whether it is safe to go or not when you get to the end of the side road. This decision will be influenced by your zone of vision (the amount of the new road you can see to either the left or the right as you approach the junction). Your zone of vision can be limited by parked vehicles, buildings, bends, hills, traffic on the main road, trees, hedges, walls and fences.

As you approach the junction your zone of vision usually improves, but it can be blocked by parked cars. In cases where there is reduced visibility you can only decide when it is safe to emerge by edging forward very slowly, looking both ways, into a position where your zone of vision is improved.

Similarly any vehicles turning left into the side road, particularly large vehicles, can hide other vehicles travelling behind or alongside them. Always take extra care at junctions where visibility is reduced.

Emerging at Y junctions

The procedure for approaching and emerging from Y junctions is basically the same as T-junctions. However, the position of the vehicle may need to be slightly different just prior to emerging to make emerging safer and extra observations must be taken as the windscreen pillars of the car may obscure your view and may cause you to miss something small like a motorcycle.

Emerging at unmarked crossroads

Neither road is the major road and therefore no one has priority. Consequently you must slow down on approach and be prepared to stop. Priority regarding oncoming vehicles is not changed, if you are turning right you would need to give way to oncoming traffic turning left or going straight ahead. If you come across a crossroad where the traffic lights have failed you should treat this as a unmarked crossroad, slow down on approach, look both ways and be prepared to stop.

When you want to pull up on the left just after a junction on the left be very careful not to mislead anyone with your signal. You should indicate left just as you pass the junction and not before it.

25. Motorcyclists and Cyclists

Motorcycles and pedal cycles are not as large or as wide as a car and as such are much more difficult to see. Many accidents happen because drivers do not notice them, particularly at junctions. So always be on the look out for them. When driving in slow moving queues of traffic motorcyclists and pedal cyclists sometimes ride between the lanes. Before you change lanes make sure you have checked for motorcyclists and pedal cycles filtering through the traffic. The windscreen and door pillows can easily hide motor and pedal cyclists so be particularly aware of the blind spots these create.

26. Following Other Vehicles

When following any vehicle always leave a safe gap between your vehicle and the one in front.

When following a large vehicle, such as a lorry or double decker bus, always keep well back, even when travelling slowly. This will allow you a better view of what is happening in front of the lorry and you will be able to judge when or if you can overtake it safely. Keeping well back also allows the driver of the lorry to see you in their mirrors. If you cannot see the mirrors on the lorry then the driver cannot see you.

It may be that you find yourself being followed very closely by another vehicle (tailgating). This can make you feel uneasy and pressured into going faster in an effort to get away from it. If this happens try to stay calm and do not speed up as the following driver will only speed up as well. If you can do so safely allow them to overtake. Sometimes this is not possible so the safest thing you can do is to gradually allow the gap between your vehicle and the one in front to increase to double what it should be by gradually slowing down. This will then give you more time to slow down or stop, should the need arise, without putting yourself in too much danger.

When driving in areas where traffic calming measures are in existence, you should reduce your speed particularly on roads which have speed humps on them. You should not attempt to overtake another vehicle within these areas and you are advised when following other vehicles, to slow down and stay behind them.

27. Dead Ground

Dead ground is a section of road that is hidden in
a dip. Vehicles in this dip cannot be seen so care must be taken before overtaking to ensure there are no areas of dead ground hiding the oncoming traffic.

28. Humpback Bridge

This type of bridge is found mainly on rural roads where the road goes over a stream or a river. The 'hump' can be quite high and will sometimes hide an oncoming vehicle from view. Consider using the horn to warn any other road users of your presence before you start to go over the bridge particularly if the road is narrow. You should slow down. Also listen out for the horns of other vehicles warning you and particularly watch for pedestrians using the bridge.

29. Priorities

The Highway Code says that where there is an obstruction on your side of the road, such as a parked car, you should give way to oncoming traffic. However sometimes common sense and courtesy should prevail and the advice of the Highway Code altered to suit the situation. For example, if you are travelling downhill and a large heavy vehicle is travelling uphill with an obstruction on their side of the road, you should give way to the lorry allowing them to continue up the hill without stopping if it is safe to do so. It is far easier for you to restart downhill than it is for the lorry going uphill.

30. Bad Weather

If you have to travel in foggy conditions always allow extra time for your journey as you will have to drive slower and so it will take you longer to reach your destination. Use dipped headlights, even in daytime fog, and if visibility is reduced to less than 100 metres use your fog lamps. When driving in clear daylight remember to turn your front and rear fog lamps off when they are no longer needed or they will dazzle other drivers. If it is foggy and your journey is not essential, stay in.

In deep snow special wheel chains can be fitted to help prevent skidding.

31 Security

If possible you should always park your car in the garage if you have one. This is the safest place for it. Failing this you should look to park your car in a secure car park. If you do have to park your car on the street try to look for a prominent position where the car is very visible. At night make sure the area is also well lit. If you have a local vehicle watch scheme in operation join this so that you can help to protect your car when parked near your home. If you install a car radio/CD/DVD make sure it is security coded.

32. Pedestrian Crossings

There are four main types of pedestrian crossing. These are the zebra crossing, pelican crossing, puffin crossing and the toucan crossing. Pelican, puffin and toucan crossings are controlled by traffic lights. Even if a traffic light is on green you should always be prepared to stop, particularly, if pedestrians have been waiting for sometime and as a consequence you suspect that the green light may shortly change to red.

Puffin crossing is the newest type of crossing and the least described in the Highway Code. Hence we will describe this crossing in more detail here.

A puffin crossing is signal controlled. The sequence of the lights is the same as normal traffic lights. They are also operated using a push button. However they also have a sensor which detects when someone is within the crossing area. Once activated the lights will not go back to green until the crossing area is clear of people and they have reached a safe position, which will be detected by the sensor.

You should also pay special attention to certain types of pedestrian who are particularly at risk when crossing the road. For example, pedestrians over 60 and those under 15, pedestrians who have disabilities or who may be deaf and/or blind. If you see a pedestrian with a dog which has a bright yellow coat, collar and lead then this informs you that the pedestrian is deaf. If the person is carrying a white stick they are blind and if they are carrying a white stick with a red band they are blind and deaf.

33. Night-time Driving
At night you will not be able to see as far as you can in daylight and so the way you drive must change to allow for the conditions. Make sure you switch on your vehicle lights so you can see and be seen. Only use main beam headlights on roads without street lamps. These lights are very bright and can dazzle the drivers of oncoming vehicles or vehicles in front so switch to dipped headlights if another vehicle approaches you or overtakes you. If a vehicle is overtaking (and there is no oncoming traffic) do not dip your headlights until the vehicle passes you. Your main beam will help the overtaking vehicle to see if there are any hazards up ahead that would make the manoeuvre unsafe. Beware of bends if you overtake anything. It is difficult to see as far in the dark and it is not easy to judge distances.

When waiting in a traffic queue at a junction use the handbrake and do not keep your foot on the brake pedal as the lights can dazzle the driver behind.

34. Motorways
Once you have passed your driving test you are allowed to drive on the motorway. The traffic travels faster which means that conditions change rapidly. You need to be alert and have total concentration. Continuous high speeds may increase the risk of your vehicle breaking down so remember to particularly check your vehicle carefully before you embark on a long motorway journey.

As you join the motorway the slip road may be divided into lanes or separated from the main carriageway by white chevron road marking. You must not cross the solid white line; it is there to keep the lanes of traffic separate. If you are travelling along the left hand lane of a motorway and you see vehicles ahead joining from a slip road be prepared to move into another lane to help the merging traffic.

You must not stop on the motorway except in an emergency, in which case use the hard shoulder. Emergency telephones are located along the edge of the motorway approximately 1 mile apart. They are connected to police control who can locate you from the number on the box. If you break down use the emergency telephone not a mobile telephone as you may not know exactly where you are. To find the nearest emergency telephone look for the small marker posts which will have an arrow on them pointing in the direction of the closest one. When using an emergency telephone always face the oncoming traffic.

If you see a car on the hard shoulder displaying a HELP pennant this means the driver is disabled and may need assistance in calling for the breakdown services.

1. Rules for motorcyclists and drivers

Before completing quiz 1 read Highway Code rules 5, 25, 33, 65, 69, 72-84.

Question: 1.1

At night you see a pedestrian wearing reflective clothing and carrying a bright red light. What does this mean?

Mark one answer

a) You are approaching roadworks
b) You are approaching an organised walk
c) You are approaching a slow-moving vehicle
d) You are approaching an accident black spot

HC rule 5

Question: 1.2

At toucan crossings

Mark two answers

a) there is no flashing amber light
b) cyclists are not permitted
c) there is a continuously flashing amber beacon
d) pedestrians and cyclists may cross
e) you only stop if someone is waiting to cross

HC rules 25 65 175

Question: 1.3

The left hand pavement is closed due to street repairs. What should you do?

Mark one answer

a) Watch out for pedestrians walking in the road
b) Use your right hand mirror more often
c) Speed up to get past the road works quicker
d) Position close to the left hand kerb

HC rule 33

Question: 1.4

At toucan crossings, apart from pedestrians you should be aware of

Mark one answer

a) emergency vehicles emerging
b) buses pulling out
c) trams crossing in front
d) cyclists riding across

HC rule 65

Question: 1.5

A toucan crossing is different from other crossings because

Mark one answer

a) moped riders can use it
b) it is controlled by a traffic warden
c) it is controlled by two flashing lights
d) cyclists can use it

HC rule 65

Question: 1.6

At which type of crossing are cyclists allowed to ride across with pedestrians?

Mark one answer

a) Toucan
b) Puffin
c) Pelican
d) Zebra

HC rule 65

Question: 1.7

Who can use a toucan crossing?

Mark two answers

a) Trains
b) Cyclists
c) Buses
d) Pedestrians
e) Trams

HC rule 65

Question: 1.8

In daylight, an approaching motorcyclist is using a dipped headlight. Why?

Mark one answer

a) So that the rider can be seen more easily
b) To stop the battery overcharging
c) To improve the rider's vision
d) The rider is inviting you to proceed

HC rule 69

Question: 1.9

Motorcyclists should wear bright clothing mainly because

Mark one answer

a) they must do so by law
b) it helps keep them cool in summer
c) the colours are popular
d) drivers often do not see them

HC rule 69

Question: 1.10

A properly adjusted head restraint will

Mark one answer

a) make you more comfortable
b) help you to avoid neck injury
c) help you to relax
d) help you to maintain your driving position

HC rule 73

Question: 1.11

It is important to wear suitable shoes when you are driving. Why is this?

Mark one answer

a) To prevent wear on the pedals
b) To maintain control of the pedals
c) To enable you to adjust your seat
d) To enable you to walk for assistance if you break down

HC rule 73

Question: 1.12

What will reduce the risk of neck injury resulting from a collision?

Mark one answer

a) An air-sprung seat
b) Anti-lock brakes
c) A collapsible steering wheel
d) A properly adjusted head restraint

HC rule 73

Question: 1.13
If a trailer swerves or snakes when you are towing it you should
Mark one answer
a) ease off the accelerator and reduce your speed
b) let go of the steering wheel and let it correct itself
c) brake hard and hold the pedal down
d) increase your speed as quickly as possible
HC rule 74

Question: 1.14
Any load that is carried on a roof rack MUST be
Mark one answer
a) securely fastened when driving
b) carried only when strictly necessary
c) as light as possible
d) covered with plastic sheeting
HC rule 74

Question: 1.15
You are towing a caravan along a motorway. The caravan begins to swerve from side to side. What should you do?
Mark one answer
a) Ease off the accelerator slowly
b) Steer sharply from side to side
c) Do an emergency stop
d) Speed up very quickly
HC rule 74

Question: 1.16
Who is responsible for making sure that a vehicle is not overloaded?
Mark one answer
a) The driver of the vehicle
b) The owner of the items being carried
c) The person who loaded the vehicle
d) The licensing authority
HC rule 74

Question: 1.17
Overloading your vehicle can seriously affect the
Mark two answers
a) gearbox
b) steering
c) handling
d) battery life
e) journey time
HC rule 74

Question: 1.18
How can you stop a caravan snaking from side to side?
Mark one answer
a) Turn the steering wheel slowly to each side
b) Accelerate to increase your speed
c) Stop as quickly as you can
d) Slow down very gradually
HC rule 74

Question: 1.19
A child under three years is being carried in your vehicle. They should be secured in a restraint. Which of these is suitable?
Mark one answer
a) An adult holding a child
b) A lap belt
c) A baby carrier
d) An adult seat belt
HC rule 75

Question: 1.20
Car passengers MUST wear a seat belt if one is available, unless they are
Mark one answer
a) under 14 years old
b) under 1.5 metres (5 feet) in height
c) sitting in the rear seat
d) exempt for medical reasons
HC rule 75

Question: 1.21
You are carrying two 13 year old children and their parents in your car. Who is responsible for seeing that the children wear seat belts?
Mark one answer
a) The children's parents
b) You, the driver
c) The front-seat passenger
d) The children
HC rule 76

Question: 1.22
You are driving a friend's children home from school. They are both under 14 years old. Who is responsible for making sure they wear a seat belt?
Mark one answer
a) An adult passenger
b) The children
c) You, the driver
d) Your friend
HC rule 76

Question: 1.23
Which of these is a suitable restraint for a child under three years?
Mark one answer
a) A child seat
b) An adult holding a child
c) An adult seat belt
d) A lap belt
HC rule 78

Question: 1.24
Rear facing baby seats should NEVER be used on a seat protected with
Mark one answer
a) an airbag
b) seat belts
c) head restraints
d) seat covers
HC rule 78

Question: 1.25

After passing your driving test, you suffer from ill health. This affects your driving. You MUST

Mark one answer

a) inform your local police station

b) get on as best you can

c) not inform anyone as you hold a full licence

d) inform the licensing authority

HC rule 79

Question: 1.26

You must notify the licensing authority when

Mark three answers

a) your health affects your driving

b) your eyesight does not meet a set standard

c) you intend lending your vehicle

d) your vehicle requires an MOT certificate

e) you change your vehicle

HC rules 79 81

Question: 1.27

During periods of illness your ability to drive may be impaired. You MUST

Mark two answers

a) see your doctor each time before you drive

b) only take smaller doses of any medicines

c) be medically fit to drive

d) not drive after taking certain medicines

e) take all your medicines with you when you drive

HC rules 79 84

Question: 1.28

As a driver you find that your eyesight has become very poor. Your optician says they cannot help you. The law says that you should tell

Mark one answer

a) the licensing authority

b) your own doctor

c) the local police station

d) another optician

HC rules 79 81 83

Question: 1.29

You are on a motorway. You feel tired. You should

Mark one answer

a) carry on but go slowly

b) leave the motorway at the next exit

c) complete your journey as quickly as possible

d) stop on the hard shoulder

HC rules 80 236

Question: 1.30

You feel drowsy when driving. You should

Mark two answers

a) stop and rest as soon as possible

b) turn the heater up to keep you warm and comfortable

c) make sure you have a good supply of fresh air

d) continue with your journey but drive more slowly

e) close the car windows to help you concentrate

HC rule 80

Question: 1.31

What else can seriously affect your concentration, other than alcoholic drinks?

Mark three answers

a) Drugs

b) Tiredness

c) Tinted windows

d) Contact lenses

e) Loud music

HC rules 80 84 126

Question: 1.32

You start to feel tired while driving. What should you do?

Mark one answer

a) Increase your speed slightly

b) Decrease your speed slightly

c) Find a less busy route

d) Pull over at a safe place to rest

HC rule 80

Question: 1.33

Which TWO things would help to keep you alert during a long journey?

Mark two answers

a) Finishing your journey as fast as you can

b) Keeping off the motorways and using country roads

c) Making sure that you get plenty of fresh air

d) Making regular stops for refreshments

HC rules 80 236

Question: 1.34

Driving long distances can be tiring. You can prevent this by

Mark three answers

a) stopping every so often for a walk

b) opening a window for some fresh air

c) ensuring plenty of refreshment breaks

d) completing the journey without stopping

e) eating a large meal before driving

HC rule 80

Question: 1.35

If your motorway journey seems boring and you feel drowsy whilst driving you should

Mark one answer

a) open a window and drive to the next service area

b) stop on the hard shoulder for a sleep

c) speed up to arrive at your destination sooner

d) slow down and let other drivers overtake

HC rules 80 236

Question: 1.36

If you are feeling tired it is best to stop as soon as you can. Until then you should

Mark one answer

a) increase your speed to find a stopping place quickly
b) ensure a supply of fresh air
c) gently tap the steering wheel
d) keep changing speed to improve concentration

HC rule 80

Question: 1.37

You are planning a long journey. Do you need to plan rest stops?

Mark one answer

a) Yes, you should plan to stop every half an hour
b) Yes, regular stops help concentration
c) No, you will be less tired if you get there as soon as possible
d) No, only fuel stops will be needed

HC rule 80

Question: 1.38

You are about to drive home. You feel very tired and have a severe headache. You should

Mark one answer

a) wait until you are fit and well before driving
b) drive home, but take a tablet for headaches
c) drive home if you can stay awake for the journey
d) wait for a short time, then drive home slowly

HC rule 80

Question: 1.39

On a long motorway journey boredom can cause you to feel sleepy. You should

Mark two answers

a) leave the motorway and find a safe place to stop
b) keep looking around at the surrounding landscape
c) drive faster to complete your journey sooner
d) ensure a supply of fresh air into your vehicle
e) stop on the hard shoulder for a rest

HC rules 80 236

Question: 1.40

You are driving along a motorway and become tired. You should

Mark two answers

a) stop at the next service area and rest
b) leave the motorway at the next exit and rest
c) increase your speed and turn up the radio volume
d) close all your windows and set heating to warm
e) pull up on the hard shoulder and change drivers

HC rules 80 236

Question: 1.41

You are travelling on a motorway. You decide you need a rest. You should

Mark two answers

a) stop on the hard shoulder
b) go to a service area
c) park on the slip road
d) park on the central reservation
e) leave at the next exit

HC rules 80 236

Question: 1.42

You find that you need glasses to read vehicle number plates at the required distance. When MUST you wear them?

Mark one answer

a) Only in bad weather conditions
b) At all times when driving
c) Only when you think it necessary
d) Only in bad light or at night time

HC rule 81

Question: 1.43

You are about to drive home. You cannot find the glasses you need to wear. You should

Mark one answer

a) drive home slowly, keeping to quiet roads
b) borrow a friend's glasses and use those
c) drive home at night, so that the lights will help you
d) find a way of getting home without driving

HC rule 81

Question: 1.44

Before entering a tunnel it is good advice to

Mark one answer

a) put on your sunglasses
b) check tyre pressures
c) change to a lower gear
d) tune your radio to a local channel

HC rule 82

Question: 1.45

Before driving through a tunnel what should you do?

Mark one answer

a) Switch your radio off
b) Remove any sunglasses
c) Close your sunroof
d) Switch on windscreen wipers

HC rule 82

Question: 1.46

Which of the following types of glasses should NOT be worn when driving at night?

Mark one answer

a) Half-moon
b) Round
c) Bi-focal
d) Tinted

HC rule 82

Question: 1.47

You go to a social event and need to drive a short time after. What precaution should you take?

Mark one answer

a) Avoid drinking alcohol on an empty stomach
b) Drink plenty of coffee after drinking alcohol
c) Avoid drinking alcohol completely
d) Drink plenty of milk before drinking alcohol

HC rule 83

Question: 1.48

Which THREE result from drinking alcohol ?

Mark three answers

a) Less control
b) A false sense of confidence
c) Faster reactions
d) Poor judgement of speed
e) Greater awareness of danger

HC rule 83

Question: 1.49

Drinking any amount of alcohol is likely to

Mark three answers

a) slow down your reactions to hazards
b) increase the speed of your reactions
c) worsen your judgement of speed
d) improve your awareness of danger
e) give a false sense of confidence

HC rule 83

Question: 1.50

Which THREE of these are likely effects of drinking alcohol?

Mark three answers

a) Reduced co-ordination
b) Increased confidence
c) Poor judgement
d) Increased concentration
e) Faster reactions
f) Colour blindness

HC rule 83

Question: 1.51

What advice should you give to a driver who has had a few alcoholic drinks at a party?

Mark one answer

a) Have a strong cup of coffee and then drive home
b) Drive home carefully and slowly
c) Go home by public transport
d) Wait a short while and then drive home

HC rule 83

Question: 1.52

You are invited to a pub lunch. You know that you will have to drive in the evening. What is your best course of action?

Mark one answer

a) Avoid mixing your alcoholic drinks
b) Not drink any alcohol at all
c) Have some milk before drinking alcohol
d) Eat a hot meal with your alcoholic drinks

HC rule 83

Question: 1.53

How does alcohol affect you?

Mark one answer

a) It speeds up your reactions
b) It increases your awareness
c) It improves your co-ordination
d) It reduces your concentration

HC rule 83

Question: 1.54

You are about to return home from holiday when you become ill. A doctor prescribes drugs which are likely to affect your driving. You should

Mark one answer

a) drive only if someone is with you
b) avoid driving on motorways
c) not drive yourself
d) never drive at more than 30 mph

HC rule 84

Question: 1.55

You have been taking medicine for a few days which made you feel drowsy. Today you feel better but still need to take the medicine. You should only drive

Mark one answer

a) if your journey is necessary
b) at night on quiet roads
c) if someone goes with you
d) after checking with your doctor

HC rule 84

Question: 1.56

You take some cough medicine given to you by a friend. What should you do before driving?

Mark one answer

a) Ask your friend if taking the medicine affected their driving
b) Drink some strong coffee one hour before driving
c) Check the label to see if the medicine will affect your driving
d) Drive a short distance to see if the medicine is affecting your driving

HC rule 84

Question: 1.57

Your doctor has given you a course of medicine. Why should you ask how it will affect you?

Mark one answer

a) Drugs make you a better driver by quickening your reactions
b) You will have to let your insurance company know about the medicine
c) Some types of medicine can cause your reactions to slow down
d) The medicine you take may affect your hearing

HC rule 84

Question: 1.58

You are taking drugs that are likely to affect your driving. What should you do?

Mark one answer

a) Seek medical advice before driving
b) Limit your driving to essential journeys
c) Only drive if accompanied by a full licence-holder
d) Drive only for short distances

HC rule 84

Question: 1.59

You are not sure if your cough medicine will affect you. What TWO things could you do?

Mark two answers

a) Ask your doctor
b) Check the medicine label
c) Drive if you feel alright
d) Ask a friend or relative for advice

HC rule 84

2. General rules part 1
Before completing quiz 2 read Highway Code rules 85 - 105.

Question: 2.1

Signals are normally given by direction indicators and

Mark one answer

a) brake lights
b) side lights
c) fog lights
d) interior lights

HC rule 85

Question: 2.2

Your indicators may be difficult to see in bright sunlight. What should you do?

Mark one answer

a) Put your indicator on earlier
b) Give an arm signal as well as using your indicator
c) Touch the brake several times to show the stop lights
d) Turn as quickly as you can

HC rule 85

Question: 2.3

You are signalling to turn right in busy traffic. How would you confirm your intention safely?

Mark one answer

a) Sound the horn
b) Give an arm signal
c) Flash your headlights
d) Position over the centre line

HC rule 85

Question: 2.4

Why should you make sure that your indicators have been cancelled after turning?

Mark one answer

a) To avoid flattening the battery
b) To avoid misleading other road users
c) To avoid dazzling other road users
d) To avoid damage to the indicator relay

HC rule 85

Question: 2.5

You think the driver of the vehicle in front has forgotten to cancel the right indicator. You should

Mark one answer

a) flash your lights to alert the driver
b) sound your horn before overtaking
c) overtake on the left if there is room
d) stay behind and not overtake

HC rules 86 143

Question: 2.6

You are waiting at a T-junction. A vehicle is coming from the right with the left signal flashing. What should you do?

Mark one answer

a) Move out and accelerate hard
b) Wait until the vehicle starts to turn in
c) Pull out before the vehicle reaches the junction
d) Move out slowly

HC rule 86

Question: 2.7

You MUST stop when signalled to do so by which THREE of these?

Mark three answers

a) A police officer
b) A pedestrian
c) A school crossing patrol
d) A bus driver
e) A red traffic light

HC rules 87 89 151

Question:　2.8

On which THREE occasions MUST you stop your vehicle?

Mark three answers

a) When involved in an accident
b) At a red traffic light
c) When signalled to do so by a police officer
d) At a junction with double broken white lines
e) At a pelican crossing when the amber light is flashing and no pedestrians are crossing

HC rules 89 151 260

Question:　2.9

There is a police car following you. The police officer flashes the headlights and points to the left. What should you do?

Mark one answer

a) Turn at the next left
b) Pull up on the left
c) Stop immediately
d) Move over to the left

HC rule 89

Question:　2.10

How will a police officer in a patrol vehicle normally get you to stop?

Mark one answer

a) Flash the headlights, indicate left and point to the left
b) Wait until you stop, then approach you
c) Use the siren, overtake, cut in front and stop
d) Pull alongside you, use the siren and wave you to stop

HC rule 89

Question:　2.11

Other drivers may sometimes flash their headlights at you. In which situation are they allowed to do this?

Mark one answer

a) To warn of a radar speed trap ahead
b) To show that they are giving way to you
c) To warn you of their presence
d) To let you know there is a fault with your vehicle

HC rule 90

Question:　2.12

You should ONLY flash your headlights to other road users

Mark one answer

a) to show that you are giving way
b) to show that you are about to turn
c) to tell them that you have right of way
d) to let them know that you are there

HC rule 90

Question:　2.13

You are travelling at the legal speed limit. A vehicle comes up quickly behind, flashing its headlights. You should

Mark one answer

a) accelerate to make a gap behind you
b) touch the brakes sharply to show your brake lights
c) maintain your speed to prevent the vehicle from overtaking
d) allow the vehicle to overtake

HC rule 91

Question:　2.14

You must NOT sound your horn

Mark one answer

a) between 10 pm and 6 am in a built-up area
b) at any time in a built-up area
c) between 11.30 pm and 7 am in a built-up area
d) between 11.30 pm and 6 am on any road

HC rule 92

Question:　2.15

When may you sound the horn?

Mark one answer

a) To give you right of way
b) To attract a friend's attention
c) To warn others of your presence
d) To make slower drivers move over

HC rule 92

Question:　2.16

When should you NOT use your horn in a built-up area?

Mark one answer

a) Between 8 pm and 8 am
b) Between 9 pm and dawn
c) Between dusk and 8 am
d) Between 11.30 pm and 7 am

HC rule 92

Question:　2.17

You must not use your horn when you are stationary

Mark one answer

a) unless a moving vehicle may cause you danger
b) at any time whatsoever
c) unless it is used only briefly
d) except for signalling that you have just arrived

HC rule 92

Question:　2.18

What should you use your horn for?

Mark one answer

a) To alert others to your presence
b) To allow you right of way
c) To greet other road users
d) To signal your annoyance

HC rule 92

Question:　2.19

You are driving along this road. The driver on the left is reversing from a driveway. You should

Mark one answer

a) move to the opposite side of the road
b) drive through as you have priority
c) sound your horn and be prepared to stop
d) speed up and drive through quickly

HC rule 92

Question: 2.20
You are driving on a clear night. There is a steady stream of oncoming traffic. The national speed limit applies. Which lights should you use?
Mark one answer
a) Full beam headlights
b) Sidelights
c) Dipped headlights
d) Fog lights
HC rules 93 95

Question: 2.21
You are on a motorway at night with other vehicles just ahead of you. Which lights should you have on?
Mark one answer
a) Front fog lights
b) Main beam headlights
c) Sidelights only
d) Dipped headlights
HC rules 93 95

Question: 2.22
You are on a well-lit motorway at night. You must
Mark one answer
a) use only your sidelights
b) always use your headlights
c) always use rear fog lights
d) use headlights only in bad weather
HC rule 93

Question: 2.23
Daytime visibility is poor but not seriously reduced. You should switch on
Mark one answer
a) headlights and fog lights
b) front fog lights
c) dipped headlights
d) rear fog lights
HC rules 93 95

Question: 2.24
You are driving with your front fog lights switched on. Earlier fog has now cleared. What should you do?

Mark one answer
a) Leave them on if other drivers have their lights on
b) Switch them off as long as visibility remains good
c) Flash them to warn oncoming traffic that it is foggy
d) Drive with them on instead of your headlights
HC rule 94

Question: 2.25
You are travelling on a well lit road at night in a built up area. By using dipped headlights you will be able to
Mark one answer
a) see further along the road
b) go at a much faster speed
c) switch to main beam quickly
d) be easily seen by others
HC rule 95

Question: 2.26
You are overtaking a car at night. You must be sure that
Mark one answer
a) you flash your headlights before overtaking
b) you select a higher gear
c) you have switched your lights to full beam before overtaking
d) you do not dazzle other road users
HC rule 95

Question: 2.27
You are driving at night on an unlit road following a slower moving vehicle. You should
Mark one answer
a) flash your headlights
b) use dipped beam headlights
c) switch off your headlights
d) use full beam headlights
HC rule 95

Question: 2.28
When MUST you use dipped headlights during the day?
Mark one answer
a) All the time
b) Along narrow streets
c) In poor visibility
d) When parking
HC rule 95

Question: 2.29
You are travelling at night. You are dazzled by headlights coming towards you. You should
Mark one answer
a) pull down your sun visor
b) slow down or stop
c) switch on your main beam headlights
d) put your hand over your eyes
HC rule 95

Question: 2.30
You are driving on a motorway. You have to slow down quickly due to a hazard. You should
Mark one answer
a) switch on your hazard lights
b) switch on your headlights
c) sound your horn
d) flash your headlights
HC rule 96

Question: 2.31
Your vehicle breaks down in a tunnel. What should you do?
Mark one answer
a) Stay in your vehicle and wait for the Police
b) Stand in the lane behind your vehicle to warn others
c) Stand in front of your vehicle to warn oncoming drivers
d) Switch on hazard lights then go and call for help immediately
HC rules 96 248

Question: 2.32
You are driving on a motorway. The traffic ahead is braking sharply because of an accident. How could you warn following traffic?
Mark one answer
a) Briefly use the hazard warning lights
b) Switch on the hazard warning lights continuously
c) Briefly use the rear fog lights
d) Switch on the headlights continuously
HC rule 96

Question: 2.33
When may you use hazard warning lights?
Mark one answer
a) To park alongside another car
b) To park on double yellow lines
c) When you are being towed
d) When you have broken down
HC rule 96

Question: 2.34
Hazard warning lights should be used when vehicles are
Mark one answer
a) broken down and causing an obstruction
b) faulty and moving slowly
c) being towed along a road
d) reversing into a side road
HC rule 96

Question: 2.35
For which TWO should you use hazard warning lights?
Mark two answers
a) When you slow down quickly on a motorway because of a hazard ahead
b) When you have broken down
c) When you wish to stop on double yellow lines
d) When you need to park on the pavement
HC rule 96

Question: 2.36
When may you use hazard warning lights when driving?
Mark one answer
a) Instead of sounding the horn in a built-up area between 11.30 pm and 7 am
b) On a motorway or unrestricted dual carriageway, to warn of a hazard ahead
c) On rural routes, after a warning sign of animals
d) On the approach to toucan crossings where cyclists are waiting to cross
HC rule 96

Question: 2.37
You are driving on a motorway. The car ahead shows its hazard lights for a short time. This tells you that
Mark one answer
a) the driver wants you to overtake
b) the other car is going to change lanes
c) traffic ahead is slowing or stopping suddenly
d) there is a police speed check ahead
HC rule 96

Question: 2.38
When are you allowed to use hazard warning lights?
Mark one answer
a) When stopped and temporarily obstructing traffic
b) When travelling during darkness without headlights
c) When parked for shopping on double yellow lines
d) When travelling slowly because you are lost
HC rule 96

Question: 2.39
For which of these may you use hazard warning lights?
Mark one answers
a) When driving on a motorway to warn traffic behind of a hazard ahead
b) When you are double-parked on a two way road
c) When your direction indicators are not working
d) When warning oncoming traffic that you intend to stop
HC rule 96

Question: 2.40
When should you use hazard warning lights?
Mark one answer
a) When you are double-parked on a two way road
b) When your direction indicators are not working
c) When warning oncoming traffic that you intend to stop
d) When your vehicle has broken down and is causing an obstruction
HC rules 96 248

Question: 2.41
You are driving through a tunnel. Your vehicle breaks down. What should you do?
Mark one answer
a) Switch on hazard warning lights
b) Remain in your vehicle
c) Wait for the police to find you
d) Rely on CCTV cameras seeing you
49
HC rules 96 148

Question: 2.42

You are turning left on a slippery road. The back of your vehicle slides to the right. You should

Mark one answer

a) brake firmly and not turn the steering wheel
b) steer carefully to the left
c) steer carefully to the right
d) brake firmly and steer to the left

HC rule 99

Question: 2.43

You are braking on a wet road. Your vehicle begins to skid. Your vehicle does not have anti-lock brakes. What is the FIRST thing you should do?

Mark one answer

a) Quickly pull up the handbrake
b) Release the footbrake fully
c) Push harder on the brake pedal
d) Gently use the accelerator

HC rule 99

Question: 2.44

What is the most common cause of skidding?

Mark one answer

a) Worn tyres
b) Driver error
c) Other vehicles
d) Pedestrians

HC rule 99

Question: 2.45

To correct a rear-wheel skid you should

Mark one answer

a) not steer at all
b) steer away from it
c) steer into it
d) apply your handbrake

HC rule 99

Question: 2.46

Skidding is mainly caused by

Mark one answer

a) the weather
b) the driver
c) the vehicle
d) the road

HC rule 99

Question: 2.47

Anti-lock brakes prevent wheels from locking. This means the tyres are less likely to

Mark one answer

a) aquaplane
b) skid
c) puncture
d) wear

HC rules 99 100

Question: 2.48

Your vehicle has anti-lock brakes, but they may not always prevent skidding. This is most likely to happen when driving

Mark two answers

a) in foggy conditions
b) on surface water
c) on loose road surfaces
d) on dry tarmac
e) at night on unlit roads

HC rules 99 100 202

Question: 2.49

You are driving a vehicle fitted with anti-lock brakes. You need to stop in an emergency. You should apply the footbrake

Mark one answer

a) slowly and gently
b) slowly but firmly
c) rapidly and gently
d) rapidly and firmly

HC rule 100

Question: 2.50

Anti-lock brakes reduce the chances of a skid occurring particularly when

Mark one answer

a) driving down steep hills
b) braking during normal driving
c) braking in an emergency
d) driving on good road surfaces

HC rule 100

Question: 2.51

Your vehicle is fitted with anti-lock brakes. To stop quickly in an emergency you should

Mark one answer

a) brake firmly and pump the brake pedal on and off
b) brake rapidly and firmly without releasing the brake pedal
c) brake gently and pump the brake pedal on and off
d) brake rapidly once, and immediately release the brake pedal

HC rule 100

Question: 2.52

Your anti-lock brakes warning light stays on. You should

Mark one answer

a) check the brake fluid level
b) check the footbrake free play
c) check that the handbrake is released
d) have the brakes checked immediately

HC rule 100

Question: 2.53

Your car is fitted with anti-lock brakes. You need to stop in an emergency. You should

Mark one answer

a) brake normally and avoid turning the steering wheel
b) press the brake pedal rapidly and firmly until you have stopped
c) keep pushing and releasing the foot brake quickly to prevent skidding
d) apply the handbrake to reduce the stopping distance

HC rule 100

The Highway Code quiz programme

Question: 2.54
Anti-lock brakes are most effective when you
Mark one answer
a) keep pumping the foot brake to prevent skidding
b) brake normally, but grip the steering wheel tightly
c) brake rapidly and firmly until you have slowed down
d) apply the handbrake to reduce the stopping distance
HC rule 100

Question: 2.55
Anti-lock brakes will take effect when
Mark one answer
a) you do not brake quickly enough
b) excessive brake pressure has been applied
c) you have not seen a hazard ahead
d) speeding on slippery road surfaces
HC rule 100

Question: 2.56
Vehicles fitted with anti-lock brakes
Mark one answer
a) are impossible to skid
b) can be steered while you are braking
c) accelerate much faster
d) are not fitted with a handbrake
HC rule 100

Question: 2.57
Anti-lock brakes are of most use when you are
Mark one answer
a) braking gently
b) driving on worn tyres
c) braking excessively
d) driving normally
HC rule 100

Question: 2.58
Driving a vehicle fitted with anti-lock brakes allows you to
Mark one answer
a) brake harder because it is impossible to skid
b) drive at higher speeds
c) steer and brake at the same time
d) pay less attention to the road ahead
HC rule 100

Question: 2.59
Anti-lock brakes can greatly assist with
Mark one answer
a) a higher cruising speed
b) steering control when braking
c) control when accelerating
d) motorway driving
HC rule 100

Question: 2.60
When would an anti-lock braking system start to work?
Mark one answer
a) After the parking brake has been applied
b) When ever pressure on the brake pedal is applied
c) Just as the wheels are about to lock
d) When the normal braking system fails to operate
HC rule 100

Question: 2.61
You have driven through a flood. What is the first thing you should do?
Mark one answer
a) Stop and check the tyres
b) Stop and dry the brakes
c) Check your exhaust
d) Test your brakes
HC rule 101

Question: 2.62
You are driving along a country road. You see this sign. AFTER dealing safely with the hazard you should always

Mark one answer
a) check your tyre pressures
b) switch on your hazard warning lights
c) accelerate briskly
d) test your brakes
HC rule 101

Question: 2.63
You have just gone through deep water. To dry off the brakes you should
Mark one answer
a) accelerate and keep to a high speed for a short time
b) go slowly while gently applying the brakes
c) avoid using the brakes at all for a few miles
d) stop for at least an hour to allow them time to dry
HC rule 101

Question: 2.64
What does this sign mean?

Mark one answer
a) Uneven road surface
b) Bridge over the road
c) Road ahead ends
d) Water across the road
HC rule 101

51

Question: 2.65
Which of the following may apply when dealing with this hazard?

Mark four answers
a) It could be more difficult in winter
b) Use a low gear and drive slowly
c) Use a high gear to prevent wheelspin
d) Test your brakes afterwards
e) Always switch on fog lamps
f) There may be a depth gauge
HC rule 101

Question: 2.66
Why should you test your brakes after this hazard?

Mark one answer
a) Because you will be on a slippery road
b) Because your brakes will be soaking wet
c) Because you will have gone down a long hill
d) Because you will have just crossed a long bridge
HC rule 101

Question: 2.67
Why is coasting wrong?
Mark one answer
a) It will cause the car to skid
b) It will make the engine stall
c) The engine will run faster
d) There is no engine braking
HC rule 102

Question: 2.68
What are TWO main reasons why coasting downhill is wrong?
Mark two answers
a) Fuel consumption will be higher
b) The vehicle will pick up speed
c) It puts more wear and tear on the tyres
d) You have less braking and steering control
e) It damages the engine
HC rule 102

Question: 2.69
Coasting the vehicle
Mark one answer
a) improves the driver's control
b) makes steering easier
c) reduces the driver's control
d) uses more fuel
HC rule 102

Question: 2.70
You are driving down a steep hill. Why could keeping the clutch down or selecting neutral for too long be dangerous?
Mark one answer
a) Fuel consumption will be higher
b) Your vehicle will pick up speed
c) It will damage the engine
d) It will wear tyres out more quickly
HC rule 102

Question: 2.71
Pressing the clutch pedal down or rolling in neutral for too long while driving will
Mark one answer
a) use more fuel
b) cause the engine to overheat
c) reduce your control
d) improve tyre wear
HC rule 102

Question: 2.72
Why could keeping the clutch down or selecting neutral for long periods of time be dangerous?
Mark one answer
a) Fuel spillage will occur
b) Engine damage may be caused
c) You will have less steering and braking control
d) It will wear tyres out more quickly
HC rule 102

Question: 2.73
A single carriageway road has this sign. What is the maximum permitted speed for a car towing a trailer?

Mark one answer
a) 30 mph
b) 40 mph
c) 50 mph
d) 60 mph
HC rule 103

Question: 2.74
You are towing a small caravan on a dual carriageway. You must not exceed

Mark one answer
a) 50 mph
b) 40 mph
c) 70 mph
d) 60 mph
HC rule 103

Question: 2.75

You are on a road that has no traffic signs. There are street lights. What is the speed limit?

Mark one answer
a) 20 mph
b) 30 mph
c) 40 mph
d) 60 mph
HC rule 103

Question: 2.76

What is the national speed limit for cars and motorcycles in the centre lane of a three-lane motorway?

Mark one answer
a) 40 mph
b) 50 mph
c) 60 mph
d) 70 mph
HC rule 103

Question: 2.77

What is the national speed limit for cars and motorcycles on a dual carriageway?

Mark one answer
a) 30 mph
b) 50 mph
c) 60 mph
d) 70 mph
HC rule 103

Question: 2.78

There are no speed limit signs on the road. How is a 30 mph limit indicated?

Mark one answer
a) By hazard warning lines
b) By street lighting
c) By pedestrian islands
d) By double or single yellow lines
HC rule 103

Question: 2.79

Where you see street lights but no speed limit signs the limit is usually

Mark one answer
a) 30 mph
b) 40 mph
c) 50 mph
d) 60 mph
HC rule 103

Question: 2.80

You are driving a car on a motorway. Unless signs show otherwise you must NOT exceed

Mark one answer
a) 50 mph
b) 60 mph
c) 70 mph
d) 80 mph
HC rule 103

Question: 2.81

You are towing a trailer on a motorway. What is your maximum speed limit?

Mark one answer
a) 40 mph
b) 50 mph
c) 60 mph
d) 70 mph
HC rule 103

Question: 2.82

You are towing a small trailer on a busy three-lane motorway. All the lanes are open. You must

Mark two answers
a) not exceed 60 mph
b) not overtake
c) have a stabiliser fitted
d) use only the left and centre lanes
HC rules 103 239

Question: 2.83

What is the maximum speed on a single carriageway road?

Mark one answer
a) 50 mph
b) 60 mph
c) 40 mph
d) 70 mph
HC rule 103

Question: 2.84

What is the national speed limit on a single carriageway road for cars and motorcycles?

Mark one answer
a) 70 mph
b) 60 mph
c) 50 mph
d) 30 mph
HC rule 103

Question: 2.85

While driving, you see this sign ahead. You should

Mark one answer
a) stop at the sign
b) slow, but continue around the bend
c) slow to a crawl and continue
d) stop and look for open farm gates
HC rules 104 124

Question: 2.86

When approaching this hazard why should you slow down?

Mark two answers
a) Because of the bend
b) Because its hard to see to the right
c) Because of approaching traffic
d) Because of animals crossing
e) Because of the level crossing
HC rule 104

Question: 2.87
What is the shortest stopping distance at 70 mph?

Mark one answer
a) 53 metres (175 feet)
b) 60 metres (197 feet)
c) 73 metres (240 feet)
d) 96 metres (315 feet)
HC rule 105

Question: 2.88
You are following a vehicle on a wet road. You should leave a time gap of at least

Mark one answer
a) one second
b) two seconds
c) three seconds
d) four seconds
HC rule 105

Question: 2.89
You are on a fast, open road in good conditions. For safety, the distance between you and the vehicle in front should be

Mark one answer
a) a two-second time gap
b) one car length
c) 2 metres (6feet 6inches)
d) two car lengths
HC rule 105

Question: 2.90
Following this vehicle too closely is unwise because

Mark one answer
a) your brakes will overheat
b) your view ahead is increased
c) your engine will overheat
d) your view ahead is reduced
HC rules 105 140

Question: 2.91
You are on a good, dry road surface. Your vehicle has good brakes and tyres. What is the BRAKING distance at 50 mph?

Mark one answer
a) 38 metres (125 feet)
b) 14 metres (46 feet)
c) 24 metres (79 feet)
d) 55 metres (180 feet)
HC rule 105

Question: 2.92
You could use the 'Two-Second Rule'

Mark one answer
a) before restarting the engine after it has stalled
b) to keep a safe gap from the vehicle in front
c) before using the 'Mirror-Signal-Manoeuvre' routine
d) when emerging on wet roads
HC rule 105

Question: 2.93
The traffic ahead of you in the left lane is slowing. You should

Mark two answers
a) be wary of cars on your right cutting in
b) accelerate past the vehicles in the left lane
c) pull up on the left hand verge
d) move across and continue in the right hand lane
e) slow down keeping a safe separation distance
HC rule 105

Question: 2.94
What is the shortest overall stopping distance on a dry road from 60 mph?

Mark one answer
a) 53 metres (175 feet)
b) 58 metres (190 feet)
c) 73 metres (240 feet)
d) 96 metres (315 feet)
HC rule 105

Question: 2.95
You are on a good, dry, road surface and your vehicle has good brakes and tyres. What is the typical overall stopping distance at 40 mph?

Mark one answer
a) 23 metres (75 feet)
b) 36 metres (120 feet)
c) 53 metres (175 feet)
d) 96 metres (315 feet)
HC rule 105

Question: 2.96

A two-second gap between yourself and the car in front is sufficient when conditions are

Mark one answer
a) wet
b) good
c) damp
d) foggy
HC rule 105

Question: 2.97

Which THREE of the following will affect your stopping distance?

Mark three answers
a) How fast you are going
b) The tyres on your vehicle
c) The time of day
d) The weather
e) The street lighting
HC rule 105

Question: 2.98

You are travelling at 50 mph on a good, dry road. What is your shortest overall stopping distance?

Mark one answer
a) 36 metres (120 feet)
b) 53 metres (175 feet)
c) 75 metres (245 feet)
d) 96 metres (315 feet)
HC rule 105

3. General rules part 2

Before completing quiz 3 read Highway Code rules 106 - 134.

Question: 3.1

The white line painted in the centre of the road means

Mark one answer
a) oncoming vehicles have priority over you
b) you should give priority to oncoming vehicles
c) there is a hazard ahead of you
d) the area is a national speed limit zone
HC rule 106

Question: 3.2

A white line like this along the centre of the road is a

Mark one answer
a) bus lane marking
b) hazard warning
c) give way marking
d) lane marking
HC rule 106

Question: 3.3

What does this road marking mean?

Mark one answer
a) Do not cross the line
b) No stopping allowed
c) You are approaching a hazard
d) No overtaking allowed
HC rule 106

Question: 3.4

Which is a hazard warning line?

Mark one answer
a) Sign A
b) Sign B
c) Sign C
d) Sign D
HC rule 106

Question: 3.5

When may you cross a double solid white line in the middle of the road?

Mark one answer

a) To pass traffic that is queuing back at a junction
b) To pass a car signalling to turn left ahead
c) To pass a road maintenance vehicle travelling at 10 mph or less
d) To pass a vehicle that is towing a trailer

HC rules 107 108

Question: 3.6

Where on a motorway would you find green reflective studs?

Mark one answer

a) Separating driving lanes
b) Between the hard shoulder and the carriageway
c) At slip road entrances and exits
d) Between the carriageway and the central reservation

HC rule 111

Question: 3.7

You are on a motorway in fog. The left-hand edge of the motorway can be identified by reflective studs. What colour are they?

Mark one answer

a) Green
b) Amber
c) Red
d) White

HC rule 111

Question: 3.8

On a motorway the amber reflective studs can be found between

Mark one answer

a) the hard shoulder and the carriageway
b) the acceleration lane and the carriageway
c) the central reservation and the carriageway
d) each pair of the lanes

HC rule 111

Question: 3.9

What colour are the reflective studs between the lanes on a motorway?

Mark one answer

a) Green
b) Amber
c) White
d) Red

HC rule 111

Question: 3.10

What colour are the reflective studs between a motorway and its slip road?

Mark one answer

a) Amber
b) White
c) Green
d) Red

HC rule 111

Question: 3.11

Where can you find reflective amber studs on a motorway?

Mark one answer

a) Separating the slip road from the motorway
b) On the left-hand edge of the road
c) On the right-hand edge of the road
d) Separating the lanes

HC rule 111

Question: 3.12

You are on a motorway. What colour are the reflective studs on the left of the carriageway?

Mark one answer

a) Green
b) Red
c) White
d) Amber

HC rule 111

Question: 3.13

You are on a three-lane motorway. There are red reflective studs on your left and white ones to your right. Where are you?

Mark one answer

a) In the right-hand lane
b) In the middle lane
c) On the hard shoulder
d) In the left-hand lane

HC rule 111

Question: 3.14

Why are destination markings painted on the road surface?

Mark one answer

a) To restrict the flow of traffic
b) To warn you of oncoming traffic
c) To enable you to change lanes early
d) To prevent you changing lanes

HC rules 113 121

Question: 3.15

Some two way roads are divided into three lanes. Why are these particularly dangerous ?

Mark one answer

a) Traffic in both directions can use the middle lane to overtake
b) Traffic can travel faster in poor weather conditions
c) Traffic can overtake on the left
d) Traffic uses the middle lane for emergencies only

HC rule 114

Question: 3.16

When may you NOT overtake on the left?

Mark one answer

a) On a free-flowing motorway or dual carriageway
b) When the traffic is moving slowly in queues
c) On a one-way street
d) When the car in front is signalling to turn right

HC rules 116 121 139

Question: 3.17

You are on a two-lane dual carriageway. For which TWO of the following would you use the right-hand lane?

Mark two answers

a) Turning right
b) Normal progress
c) Staying at the minimum allowed speed
d) Constant high speed
e) Overtaking slower traffic
f) Mending punctures

HC rule 116

Question: 3.18

On a three-lane dual carriageway the right-hand lane can be used for

Mark one answer

a) overtaking only, never turning right
b) overtaking or turning right
c) fast-moving traffic only
d) turning right only, never overtaking

HC rule 117

Question: 3.19

A crawler lane on a motorway is found

Mark one answer

a) on a steep gradient
b) before a service area
c) before a junction
d) along the hard shoulder

HC rule 118

Question: 3.20

What does this sign mean?

Mark one answer

a) Leave motorway at next exit
b) Lane for heavy and slow vehicles
c) All lorries use the hard shoulder
d) Rest area for lorries

HC rule 118

Question: 3.21

A cycle lane is marked by a solid white line. You must not drive or park in it

Mark one answer

a) at any time
b) during the rush hour
c) if a cyclist is using it
d) during its period of operation

HC rule 119

Question: 3.22

You are driving along a road that has a cycle lane. The lane is marked by a solid white line. This means that during its period of operation

Mark one answer

a) the lane may be used for parking your car
b) you may drive in that lane at any time
c) the lane may be used when necessary
d) you must not drive in that lane

HC rule 119

Question: 3.23
As a car driver which THREE lanes are you NOT normally allowed to use?
Mark three answers
a) Crawler lane
b) Bus lane
c) Overtaking lane
d) Acceleration lane
e) Cycle lane
f) Tram lane
HC rules 119 120

Question: 3.24
You are driving on a road that has a cycle lane. The lane is marked by a broken white line. This means that
Mark two answers
a) you should not drive in the lane unless it is unavoidable
b) you should not park in the lane unless it is unavoidable
c) you can drive in the lane at any time
d) the lane must be used by motorcyclists in heavy traffic
HC rule 119

Question: 3.25
When may you drive a motor car in this bus lane?

Mark one answer
a) Outside its hours of operation
b) To get to the front of a traffic queue
c) You may not use it at any time
d) To overtake slow-moving traffic
HC rule 120

Question: 3.26
A bus lane on your left shows no times of operation. This means it is

Mark one answer
a) not in operation at all
b) only in operation at peak times
c) in operation 24 hours a day
d) only in operation in daylight hours
HC rule 120

Question: 3.27
Where may you overtake on a one-way street?
Mark one answer
a) Only on the left-hand side
b) Overtaking is not allowed
c) Only on the right-hand side
d) Either on the right or the left
HC rule 121

Question: 3.28
You are in a one-way street and want to turn right. You should position yourself
Mark one answer
a) in the right-hand lane
b) in the left-hand lane
c) in either lane, depending on the traffic
d) just left of the centre line
HC rule 121

Question: 3.29
Where would you see a contraflow bus and cycle lane?
Mark one answer
a) On a dual carriageway
b) On a roundabout
c) On an urban motorway
d) On a one-way street
HC rule 121

Question: 3.30
You lose your way on a busy road. What is the best action to take?
Mark one answer
a) Stop at traffic lights and ask pedestrians
b) Shout to other drivers to ask them the way
c) Turn into a side road, stop and check a map
d) Check a map, and keep going with the traffic flow
HC rule 122

Question: 3.31
You may drive over a footpath
Mark one answer
a) to overtake slow-moving traffic
b) when the pavement is very wide
c) if no pedestrians are near
d) to get into a property
HC rule 123

Question: 3.32
You are driving at 60 mph. As you approach this hazard you should

Mark one answer
a) maintain your speed
b) reduce your speed
c) take the next right turn
d) take the next left turn
HC rule 124

Question: 3.33
Who has priority at an unmarked crossroads?
Mark one answer
a) The larger vehicle
b) No one has priority
c) The faster vehicle
d) The smaller vehicle
HC rule 124

Question: 3.34
At a crossroads there are no signs or road markings. Two vehicles approach. Which has priority?
Mark one answer
a) Neither of the vehicle
b) The vehicle travelling the fastest
c) Oncoming vehicles turning right
d) Vehicles approaching from the right
HC rule 124

Question: 3.35
A driver's behaviour has upset you. It may help if you
Mark one answer
a) stop and take a break
b) shout abusive language
c) gesture to them with your hand
d) follow their car, flashing the headlights
HC rule 125

Question: 3.36
A vehicle pulls out in front of you at a junction. What should you do?
Mark one answer
a) Swerve past it and sound your horn
b) Flash your headlights and drive up close behind
c) Slow down and be ready to stop
d) Accelerate past it immediately
HC rule 125

Question: 3.37
A driver pulls out of a side road in front of you. You have to brake hard. You should
Mark one answer
a) ignore the error and stay calm
b) flash your lights to show your annoyance
c) sound your horn to show your annoyance
d) overtake as soon as possible
HC rule 125

Question: 3.38
A driver does something that upsets you. You should
Mark one answer
a) try not to react
b) let them know how you feel
c) flash your headlights several times
d) sound your horn
HC rule 125

Question: 3.39
Which THREE are likely to make you lose concentration while driving?
Mark three answers
a) Looking at road maps
b) Listening to loud music
c) Using your windscreen washers
d) Looking in your wing mirror
e) Using a mobile phone
HC rules 126 127

Question: 3.40
You are most likely to lose concentration when driving if you
Mark two answers
a) use a mobile phone
b) listen to very loud music
c) switch on the heated rear window
d) look at the door mirrors
HC rules 126 127

Question: 3.41
Which FOUR are most likely to cause you to lose concentration while you are driving?
Mark four answers
a) Using a mobile phone
b) Talking into a microphone
c) Tuning your car radio
d) Looking at a map
e) Checking the mirrors
f) Using the demisters
HC rules 126 127

Question: 3.42
Which of the following may cause loss of concentration on a long journey?
Mark four answers
a) Loud music
b) Arguing with a passenger
c) Using a mobile phone
d) Putting in a cassette tape
e) Stopping regularly to rest
f) Pulling up to tune the radio
HC rules 126 127

Question: 3.43
Your vehicle is fitted with a hands free phone system. Using this equipment whilst driving
Mark one answer
a) is quite safe as long as you slow down
b) could distract your attention from the road
c) is recommended by The Highway Code
d) could be very good for road safety
HC rule 127

Question: 3.44
What is the safest way to use a mobile phone in your vehicle?
Mark one answer
a) Use hands free equipment
b) Find a suitable place to stop
c) Drive slowly on a quiet road
d) Direct your call through the operator
HC rule 127

Question: 3.45

You should ONLY use a mobile phone when

Mark one answer

a) receiving a call
b) suitably parked
c) driving at less than 30 mph
d) driving an automatic vehicle

HC rule 127

Question: 3.46

Using a mobile phone while you are driving

Mark one answer

a) is acceptable in a vehicle with power steering
b) will reduce your field of vision
c) could distract your attention from the road
d) will affect your vehicle's electronic systems

HC rule 127

Question: 3.47

Your mobile phone rings while you are on the motorway. Before answering you should

Mark one answer

a) reduce your speed to 50 mph
b) pull up on the hard shoulder
c) move into the left hand lane
d) stop in a safe place

HC rule 127

Question: 3.48

To answer a call on your mobile phone while travelling you should

Mark one answer

a) reduce your speed wherever you are
b) stop in a proper and convenient place
c) keep the call time to a minimum
d) slow down and allow others to overtake

HC rule 127

Question: 3.49

Your vehicle is fitted with a hand-held telephone. To use the telephone you should

Mark one answer

a) reduce your speed
b) find a safe place to stop
c) steer the vehicle with one hand
d) be particularly careful at junctions

HC rule 127

Question: 3.50

You should not use a mobile phone whilst driving

Mark one answer

a) until you are satisfied that no other traffic is near
b) unless you are able to drive one handed
c) because it might distract your attention from the road ahead
d) because reception is poor when the engine is running

HC rule 127

Question: 3.51

Your mobile phone rings while you are travelling. You should

Mark one answer

a) stop immediately
b) answer it immediately
c) pull up in a suitable place
d) pull up at the nearest kerb

HC rule 127

Question: 3.52

Using a hands-free phone is likely to

Mark one answer

a) improve your safety
b) increase your concentration
c) reduce your view
d) divert your attention

HC rule 127

Question: 3.53

You are going through a congested tunnel and have to stop. What should you do?

Mark one answer

a) Pull up very close to the vehicle in front to save space
b) Ignore any message signs as they are never up to date
c) Keep a safe distance from the vehicle in front
d) Make a U-turn and find another route

HC rule 129

Question: 3.54

Why should the junction on the left be kept clear?

Mark one answer

a) To allow vehicles to enter and emerge
b) To allow the bus to reverse
c) To allow vehicles to make a 'U' turn
d) To allow vehicles to park

HC rule 129

Question: 3.55
What THREE things should the driver of the grey car (arrowed) be especially aware of?

Mark three answers
a) Pedestrians stepping out between cars
b) Other cars behind the grey car
c) Doors opening on parked cars
d) The bumpy road surface
e) Cars leaving parking spaces
f) Empty parking spaces
HC rule 130

Question: 3.56
You are going along a street with parked vehicles on the left-hand side. For which THREE reasons should you keep your speed down?
Mark three answers
a) So that oncoming traffic can see you more clearly
b) You may set off car alarms
c) Vehicles may be pulling out
d) Drivers' doors may open
e) Children may run out from between the vehicles
HC rule 130

Question: 3.57
In some narrow residential streets you will find a speed limit of
Mark one answer
a) 20 mph
b) 25 mph
c) 35 mph
d) 40 mph
HC rule 130

Question: 3.58
What are TWO main hazards you should be aware of when going along this street?

Mark two answers
a) Glare from the sun
b) Car doors opening suddenly
c) Lack of road markings
d) The headlights on parked cars being switched on
e) Large goods vehicles
f) Children running out from between vehicles
HC rule 130

Question: 3.59
You are driving past parked cars. You notice a wheel of a bicycle sticking out between them. What should you do?
Mark one answer
a) Accelerate past quickly and sound your horn
b) Slow down and wave the cyclist across
c) Brake sharply and flash your headlights
d) Slow down and be prepared to stop for a cyclist
HC rule 130

Question: 3.60
Which of these plates normally appear with this road sign?

Humps for 1/2 Mile	Hump Bridge
Sign A	Sign B
Low Bridge	Soft Verge
Sign C	Sign D

Mark one answer
a) Sign A
b) Sign B
c) Sign C
d) Sign D
HC rule 131

Question: 3.61
Traffic calming measures are used to
Mark one answer
a) stop road rage
b) help overtaking
c) slow traffic down
d) help parking
HC rule 131

Question: 3.62
You enter a road where there are road humps. What should you do?

Mark one answer
a) Maintain a reduced speed throughout
b) Accelerate quickly between each one
c) Always keep to the maximum legal speed
d) Drive slowly at school times only
HC rule 131

Question: 3.63
What does this sign mean?

Mark one answer
a) Maximum speed limit with traffic calming
b) Minimum speed limit with traffic calming
c) '20 cars only' parking zone
d) Only 20 cars allowed at any one time
HC rule 131

Question: 3.64
What does this sign mean?

Mark one answer
a) New speed limit 20 mph
b) No vehicles over 30 tonnes
c) Minimum speed limit 30 mph
d) End of 20 mph zone
HC rule 131

Question: 3.65
What does this sign mean?

Mark one answer
a) Humpback bridge
b) Humps in the road
c) Entrance to tunnel
d) Soft verges
HC rule 131

Question: 3.66
Where would you see this road marking?

Mark one answer
a) At traffic lights
b) On road humps
c) Near a level crossing
d) At a box junction
HC rule 131   D
SA Category 11-116

Question: 3.67
In areas where there are 'traffic calming' measures you should
Mark one answer
a) drive at a reduced speed
b) always drive at the speed limit
c) position in the centre of the road
d) only slow down if pedestrians are near
HC rule 131

Question: 3.68
You are driving in a built-up area. You approach a speed hump. You should

Mark one answer
a) move across to the left-hand side of the road
b) wait for any pedestrians to cross
c) slow your vehicle right down
d) stop and check both pavements
HC rule 131

Question: 3.69
Road humps, chicanes, and narrowings are
Mark one answer
a) always at major road works
b) used to increase traffic speed
c) at toll-bridge approaches only
d) traffic calming measures
HC rule 131

Question: 3.70
You are on a country road. What should you expect to see coming towards you on YOUR side of the road?
Mark one answer
a) Motorcycles
b) Bicycles
c) Pedestrians
d) Horse riders
HC rules 132 2

Question: 3.71

You are driving towards this left hand bend. What dangers should you be aware of?

Mark one answer

a) A vehicle overtaking you
b) No white lines in the centre of the road
c) No sign to warn you of the bend
d) Pedestrians walking towards you
HC rules 132 2

Question: 3.72

You are driving a slow-moving vehicle on a narrow winding road. In order to let other vehicles overtake you should

Mark one answer

a) wave to them to pass
b) pull in when you can
c) show a left turn signal
d) keep left and hold your speed
HC rules 133 145

Question: 3.73

You are driving a slow moving vehicle on a narrow road. When traffic wishes to overtake you should

Mark one answer

a) take no action
b) put your hazard warning lights on
c) stop immediately and wave it on
d) pull in safely as soon as you can do so
HC rules 133 145

Question: 3.74

You are driving a slow moving vehicle on a narrow winding road. You should

Mark one answer

a) keep well out to stop vehicles overtaking dangerously
b) wave following vehicles past you if you think they can overtake quickly
c) pull in safely when you can, to let following vehicles overtake
d) give a left signal when it is safe for vehicles to overtake you
HC rules 133 145

Question: 3.75

You see a vehicle coming towards you on a single track road. You should

Mark one answer

a) go back to the main road
b) do an emergency stop
c) stop at a passing place
d) put on your hazard warning lights
HC rule 133

Question: 3.76

You are on a road that is only wide enough for one vehicle. There is a car coming towards you. What should you do?

Mark one answer

a) Pull into a passing place on your right
b) Force the other driver to reverse
c) Pull into a passing place if your vehicle is wider
d) Pull into a passing place on your left
HC rule 133

4. Using the road

Before completing quiz 4 read Highway Code rules 135 - 179.

Question: 4.1

Before you make a U-turn in the road, you should

Mark one answer

a) give an arm signal as well as using your indicators
b) signal so that other drivers can slow down for you
c) look over your shoulder for a final check
d) select a higher gear than normal
HC rule 135

Question: 4.2

When you are moving off from behind a parked car you should

Mark three answers

a) look round before you move off
b) use all the mirrors on the vehicle
c) look round after moving off
d) use the exterior mirrors only
e) give a signal if necessary
f) give a signal after moving off
HC rule 135

Question: 4.3

As a driver what does the term 'Blind Spot' mean?

Mark one answer

a) An area covered by your right hand mirror
b) An area not covered by your headlights
c) An area covered by your left hand mirror
d) An area not seen in your mirrors
HC rule 135

Question: 4.4

You are on a long, downhill slope. What should you do to help control the speed of your vehicle?

Mark one answer

a) Select neutral
b) Select a lower gear
c) Grip the handbrake firmly
d) Apply the parking brake gently
HC rule 136

Question: 4.5
When approaching a right-hand bend you should keep well to the left. Why is this?

Mark one answer
a) To improve your view of the road
b) To overcome the effect of the road's slope
c) To let faster traffic from behind overtake
d) To be positioned safely if you skid
HC rule 136

Question: 4.6
How can you use the engine of your vehicle as a brake ?
Mark one answer
a) By changing to a lower gear
b) By selecting reverse gear
c) By changing to a higher gear
d) By selecting neutral gear
HC rule 136

Question: 4.7
You are about to go down a steep hill. To control the speed of your vehicle you should
Mark one answer
a) select a high gear and use the brakes carefully
b) select a high gear and use the brakes firmly
c) select a low gear and use the brakes carefully
d) select a low gear and avoid using the brakes
HC rule 136

Question: 4.8
Which of the following should you do before stopping?
Mark one answer
a) Sound the horn
b) Use the mirrors
c) Select a higher gear
d) Flash your headlights
HC rule 137

Question: 4.9
Which TWO should you allow extra room when overtaking?
Mark two answers
a) Motorcycles
b) Tractors
c) Bicycles
d) Road-sweeping vehicles
HC rules 139 189

Question: 4.10
When you are overtaking a cyclist you should leave as much room as you would give to a car. What is the main reason for this?
Mark one answer
a) The cyclist might change lanes
b) The cyclist might get off the bike
c) The cyclist might swerve
d) The cyclist might have to make a right turn
HC rules 139 189

Question: 4.11
You should never attempt to overtake a cyclist
Mark one answer
a) just before you turn left
b) on a left hand bend
c) on a one-way street
d) on a dual carriageway
HC rules 139 158 188

Question: 4.12
It is very windy. You are about to overtake a motorcyclist. You should
Mark one answer
a) overtake slowly
b) allow extra room
c) sound your horn
d) keep close as you pass
HC rules 139 207

Question: 4.13
In which THREE of these situations may you overtake another vehicle on the left?
Mark three answers
a) When you are in a one-way street
b) When approaching a motorway slip road where you will be turning off
c) When the vehicle in front is signalling to turn right
d) When a slower vehicle is travelling in the right-hand lane of a dual carriageway
e) In slow-moving traffic queues when traffic in the right-hand lane is moving more slowly
HC rules 139 121

Question: 4.14
You are travelling along this narrow country road. When passing the cyclist you should go

Mark one answer
a) slowly, sounding the horn as you pass
b) quickly, leaving plenty of room
c) slowly, leaving plenty of room
d) quickly, sounding the horn as you pass
HC rules 139 188

Question: 4.15
You meet an obstruction on your side of the road. You should
Mark one answer
a) carry on, you have priority
b) give way to oncoming traffic
c) wave oncoming vehicles through
d) accelerate to get past first
HC rule 139

64

Question: 4.16

Why should you allow extra room when overtaking a motorcyclist on a windy day?

Mark one answer

a) The rider may turn off suddenly to get out of the wind
b) The rider may be blown across in front of you
c) The rider may stop suddenly
d) The rider may be travelling faster than normal

HC rules 139 207

Question: 4.17

Why is passing a lorry more risky than passing a car?

Mark one answer

a) Lorries are longer than cars
b) Lorries may suddenly pull up
c) The brakes of lorries are not as good
d) Lorries climb hills more slowly

HC rule 140

Question: 4.18

Before overtaking a large vehicle you should keep well back. Why is this?

Mark one answer

a) To give acceleration space to overtake quickly on blind bends
b) To get the best view of the road ahead
c) To leave a gap in case the vehicle stops and rolls back
d) To offer other drivers a safe gap if they want to overtake you

HC rule 140

Question: 4.19

You wish to overtake a long, slow moving vehicle on a busy road. You should

Mark one answer

a) follow it closely and keep moving out to see the road ahead
b) flash your headlights for the oncoming traffic to give way
c) stay behind until the driver waves you past
d) keep well back until you can see that it is clear

HC rule 140

Question: 4.20

You see this white arrow on the road ahead. It means

Mark one answer

a) entrance on the left
b) all vehicles turn left
c) keep left of the hatched markings
d) road bending to the left

HC rules 141 109

Question: 4.21

This road marking warns

Mark one answer

a) drivers to use the hard shoulder
b) overtaking drivers there is a bend to the left
c) overtaking drivers to move back to the left
d) drivers that it is safe to overtake

HC rule 141

Question: 4.22

There is a tractor ahead of you. You wish to overtake but you are NOT sure if it is safe to do so. You should

Mark one answer

a) follow another overtaking vehicle through
b) sound your horn to the slow vehicle to pull over
c) speed through but flash your lights to oncoming traffic
d) not overtake if you are in doubt

HC rule 142

Question: 4.23

You should not overtake when

Mark three answers

a) intending to turn left shortly afterwards
b) in a one-way street
c) approaching a junction
d) going up a long hill
e) the view ahead is blocked

HC rules 142 143 158

Question: 4.24

You are on a narrow road at night. A slower-moving vehicle ahead has been signalling right for some time. What should you do?

Mark one answer

a) Overtake on the left
b) Flash your headlights before overtaking
c) Signal right and sound your horn
d) Wait for the signal to be cancelled before overtaking

HC rule 143

Question: 4.25

You are following a slower-moving vehicle on a narrow country road. There is a junction just ahead on the right. What should you do?

Mark one answer

a) Overtake after checking your mirrors and signalling
b) Stay behind until you are past the junction
c) Accelerate quickly to pass before the junction
d) Slow down and prepare to overtake on the left

Supplementary note 27

Question: 4.26

You are following a long lorry. The driver signals to turn left into a narrow road. What should you do?

Mark one answer

a) Overtake on the left before the lorry reaches the junction
b) Overtake on the right as soon as the lorry slows down
c) Do not overtake unless you can see there is no oncoming traffic
d) Do not overtake, stay well back and be prepared to stop.

Supplementary note 27

Question: 4.27
You are following a large vehicle approaching crossroads. The driver signals to turn left. What should you do?
Mark one answer
a) Overtake if you can leave plenty of room.
b) Overtake only if there are no oncoming vehicles.
c) Do not overtake until the vehicle begins to turn.
d) Do not overtake when at or approaching a junction.
Supplementary note 27

Question: 4.28
You are driving in traffic at the speed limit for the road. The driver behind is trying to overtake. You should
Mark one answer
a) move closer to the car ahead, so the driver behind has no room to overtake
b) wave the driver behind to overtake when it is safe
c) keep a steady course and allow the driver behind to overtake
d) accelerate to get away from the driver behind
HC rule 144

Question: 4.29
You are following a vehicle at a safe distance on a wet road. Another driver overtakes you and pulls into the gap you have left. What should you do?
Mark one answer
a) Flash your headlights as a warning
b) Try to overtake safely as soon as you can
c) Drop back to regain a safe distance
d) Stay close to the other vehicle until it moves on
HC rule 144

Question: 4.30
A long, heavily-laden lorry is taking a long time to overtake you. What should you do?
Mark one answer
a) Speed up
b) Slow down
c) Hold your speed
d) Change direction
HC rule 144

Question: 4.31
You have just been overtaken by this motorcyclist who is cutting in sharply. You should

Mark one answer
a) sound the horn
b) brake firmly
c) keep a safe gap
d) flash your lights
HC rule 144

Question: 4.32
You are driving along this road. The red van cuts in close in front of you. What should you do?

Mark one answer
a) Accelerate to get closer to the red van
b) Give a long blast on the horn
c) Drop back to leave the correct separation distance
d) Flash your headlights several times
HC rule 144

Question: 4.33
You keep well back while waiting to overtake a large vehicle. A car fills the gap. You should
Mark one answer
a) sound your horn
b) drop back further
c) flash your headlights
d) start to overtake
HC rule 144

Question: 4.34
Where in particular should you look out for motorcyclists?

Mark one answer
a) In a filling station
b) At a road junction
c) Near a service area
d) When entering a car park
HC rules 146 187

Question: 4.35
You are about to reverse into a side road. A pedestrian wishes to cross behind you. You should
Mark one answer
a) wave to the pedestrian to stop
b) give way to the pedestrian
c) wave to the pedestrian to cross
d) reverse before the pedestrian starts to cross
HC rules 146 178

Question: 4.36
Why should you look particularly for motorcyclists and cyclists at junctions ?
Mark one answer
a) They may want to turn into the side road
b) They may slow down to let you turn
c) They are harder to see
d) They might not see you turn
HC rules 146 187

Question: 4.37
You are turning left into a side road. What hazards should you be especially aware of?

Mark one answer
a) One way street
b) Pedestrians
c) Traffic congestion
d) Parked vehicles
HC rules 146 158

Question: 4.38
You are reversing around a corner when you notice a pedestrian walking behind you. What should you do?

Mark one answer
a) Slow down and wave the pedestrian across
b) Continue reversing and steer round the pedestrian
c) Stop and give way
d) Continue reversing and sound your horn
HC rules 146 178

Question: 4.39
Where should you take particular care to look out for motorcyclists and cyclists?

Mark one answer
a) On dual carriageways
b) At junctions
c) At zebra crossings
d) On one-way streets
HC rules 146 187

Question: 4.40
What MUST you do when you see this sign?

Mark one answer
a) Stop, ONLY if traffic is approaching
b) Stop, even if the road is clear
c) Stop, ONLY if children are waiting to cross
d) Stop, ONLY if a red light is showing
HC rule 147

Question: 4.41
At this blind junction you must stop

Mark one answer
a) behind the line, then edge forward to see clearly
b) beyond the line at a point where you can see clearly
c) only if there is traffic on the main road
d) only if you are turning to the right
HC rule 147

Question: 4.42
This marking appears on the road just before a

Mark one answer
a) no entry sign
b) give way sign
c) stop sign
d) no through road sign
HC rule 148

Question: 4.43
The dual carriageway you are turning right onto has a very narrow central reserve. What should you do?

Mark one answer
a) Proceed to central reserve and wait
b) Wait until the road is clear in both directions
c) Stop in first lane so that other vehicles give way
d) Emerge slightly to show your intentions
HC rule 149

Question: 4.44
You are turning right onto a dual carriageway. What should you do before emerging?

Mark one answer
a) Stop, apply the handbrake and then select a low gear
b) Position your vehicle well to the left of the side road
c) Check that the central reserve is wide enough for your vehicle
d) Make sure that you leave enough room for a following vehicle
HC rule 149

Question: 4.45

You want to turn right at a box junction. There is oncoming traffic. You should

Mark one answer

a) wait in the box junction if your exit is clear

b) wait before the junction until it is clear of all traffic

c) drive on, you cannot turn right at a box junction

d) drive slowly into the box junction when signalled by oncoming traffic

HC rule 150

Question: 4.46

You may only enter a box junction when

Mark one answer

a) there are less than two vehicles in front of you

b) the traffic lights show green

c) your exit road is clear

d) you need to turn left

HC rule 150

Question: 4.47

You may wait in a yellow box junction when

Mark one answer

a) oncoming traffic is preventing you from turning right

b) you are in a queue of traffic turning left

c) you are in a queue of traffic to go ahead

d) you are on a roundabout

HC rule 150

Question: 4.48

What is the purpose of these yellow criss-cross lines on the road?

Mark one answer

a) To make you more aware of the traffic lights

b) To guide you into position as you turn

c) To prevent the junction from becoming blocked

d) To show you where to stop when the lights change

HC rule 150

Question: 4.49

What is the reason for the yellow criss-cross lines painted on the road here?

Mark one answer

a) To mark out an area for trams only

b) To prevent queuing traffic from blocking the junction on the left

c) To mark the entrance lane to a car park

d) To warn you of the tram lines crossing the road

HC rule 150

Question: 4.50

When may you wait in a box junction?

Mark one answer

a) When you are stationary in a queue of traffic

b) When approaching a pelican crossing

c) When approaching a zebra crossing

d) When oncoming traffic prevents you turning right

HC rule 150

Question: 4.51
A red traffic light means

Mark one answer
a) you must stop behind the white stop line
b) you may go straight on if there is no other traffic
c) you may turn left if it is safe to do so
d) you must slow down and prepare to stop if traffic has started to cross
HC rule 151

Question: 4.52
A red traffic light means

Mark one answer
a) you should stop unless turning left
b) stop, if you are able to brake safely
c) you must stop and wait behind the stop line
d) proceed with caution
HC rule 151

Question: 4.53
At traffic lights, amber on its own means

Mark one answer
a) prepare to go
b) go if the way is clear
c) go if no pedestrians are crossing
d) stop at the stop line
HC rule 151

Question: 4.54
You are approaching traffic lights. Red and amber are showing. This means

Mark one answer
a) pass the lights if the road is clear
b) there is a fault with the lights – take care
c) wait for the green light before you pass the lights
d) the lights are about to change to red
HC rule 151

Question: 4.55
When traffic lights are out of order, who has priority?
Mark one answer
a) Traffic going straight on
b) Traffic turning right
c) Nobody
d) Traffic turning left
HC rule 152

Question: 4.56
You are at a junction controlled by traffic lights. When should you NOT proceed at green?

Mark one answer
a) When pedestrians are waiting to cross
b) When your exit from the junction is blocked
c) When you think the lights may be about to change
d) When you intend to turn right
HC rule 152

Question: 4.57
You are in the left-hand lane at traffic lights. You are waiting to turn left. At which of these traffic lights must you NOT move on?

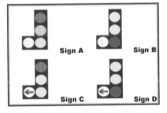

Mark one answer
a) Sign A
b) Sign B
c) Sign C
d) Sign D
HC rule 153

Question: 4.58

When the traffic lights change to green the white car should

Mark one answer

a) wait for the cyclist to pull away
b) move off quickly and turn in front of the cyclist
c) move close up to the cyclist to beat the lights
d) sound the horn to warn the cyclist

HC rule 154

Question: 4.59

You wish to turn right ahead. Why should you take up the correct position in good time?

Mark one answer

a) To allow other drivers to pull out in front of you
b) To give a better view into the road that you're joining
c) To help other road users know what you intend to do
d) To allow drivers to pass you on the right

HC rule 155

Question: 4.60

You are driving on a main road. You intend to turn right into a side road. Just before turning you should

Mark one answer

a) adjust your interior mirror
b) flash your headlamps
c) steer over to the left
d) check for traffic overtaking on your right

HC rule 156

Question: 4.61

You want to turn right from a main road into a side road. Just before turning you should

Mark one answer

a) cancel your right-turn signal
b) select first gear
c) check for traffic overtaking on your right
d) stop and set the handbrake

HC rule 156

Question: 4.62

You are at the front of a queue of traffic waiting to turn right into a side road. Why is it important to check your right mirror just before turning?

Mark one answer

a) To look for pedestrians about to cross
b) To check for overtaking vehicles
c) To make sure the side road is clear
d) To check for emerging traffic

HC rule 156

Question: 4.63

You intend to turn right into a side road. Just before turning you should check for motorcyclists who might be

Mark one answer

a) overtaking on your left
b) following you closely
c) emerging from the side road
d) overtaking on your right

HC rule 156

Question: 4.64

You are intending to turn right at a crossroads. An oncoming driver is also turning right. It will normally be safer to

Mark one answer

a) keep the other vehicle to your RIGHT and turn behind it (offside to offside)
b) keep the other vehicle to your LEFT and turn in front of it (nearside to nearside)
c) carry on and turn at the next junction instead
d) hold back and wait for the other driver to turn first

HC rule 157

Question: 4.65

You intend to turn left at the traffic lights. Just before turning you should

Mark one answer

a) check your right mirror
b) move close up to the white car
c) straddle the lanes
d) check for bicycles on your left

HC rule 158

Question: 4.66

You are following a cyclist. You wish to turn left just ahead. You should

Mark one answer

a) overtake the cyclist before the junction
b) pull alongside the cyclist and stay level until after the junction
c) hold back until the cyclist has passed the junction
d) go around the cyclist on the junction

HC rules 158 188

Question: 4.67

You are travelling behind a moped. You want to turn left just ahead. You should

Mark one answer

a) overtake the moped before the junction
b) pull alongside the moped and stay level until just before the junction
c) sound your horn as a warning and pull in front of the moped
d) stay behind until the moped has passed the junction

HC rules 158 188

Question: 4.68

While driving, you intend to turn left into a minor road. On the approach you should

Mark one answer

a) keep just left of the middle of the road
b) keep in the middle of the road
c) swing out wide just before turning
d) keep well to the left of the road

HC rule 159

Question: 4.69

You are going straight ahead at a roundabout. How should you signal?

Mark one answer

a) Signal right on the approach and then left to leave the roundabout
b) Signal left as you leave the roundabout
c) Signal left on the approach to the roundabout and keep the signal on until you leave
d) Signal left just after you pass the exit before the one you will take

HC rule 162

Question: 4.70

When going straight ahead at a roundabout you should

Mark one answer

a) indicate left before leaving the roundabout
b) not indicate at any time
c) indicate right when approaching the roundabout
d) indicate left when approaching the roundabout

HC rule 162

Question: 4.71

Which three of the following are most likely to take an unusual course at roundabouts ?

Mark three answers

a) Horse riders
b) Milk floats
c) Delivery vans
d) Long vehicles
e) Estate cars
f) Cyclists

HC rule 163

Question: 4.72

Which vehicle might have to use a different course to normal at roundabouts?

Mark one answer

a) Sports car
b) Van
c) Estate car
d) Long vehicle

HC rule 163

Question: 4.73

You see a horse rider as you approach a roundabout. They are signalling right but keeping well to the left. You should

Mark one answer

a) proceed as normal
b) keep close to them
c) cut in front of them
d) stay well back

HC rule 163

Question: 4.74

A horse rider is in the left-hand lane approaching a roundabout. You should expect the rider to

Mark one answer

a) go in any direction
b) turn right
c) turn left
d) go ahead

HC rule 163

Question: 4.75

You are coming up to a roundabout. A cyclist is signalling to turn right. What should you do?

Mark one answer

a) Overtake on the right
b) Give a horn warning
c) Signal the cyclist to move across
d) Give the cyclist plenty of room

HC rule 163

Question: 4.76

You are following two cyclists. They approach a roundabout in the left-hand lane. In which direction should you expect the cyclists to go?

Mark one answer

a) Left
b) Right
c) Any direction
d) Straight ahead

HC rules 163 62

Question: 4.77

You are approaching a roundabout. There are horses just ahead of you. You should

Mark two answers

a) be prepared to stop
b) treat them like any other vehicle
c) give them plenty of room
d) accelerate past as quickly as possible
e) sound your horn as a warning

HC rule 163

Question: 4.78

You are approaching this roundabout and see the cyclist signal right. Why is the cyclist keeping to the left?

Mark one answer

a) It is a quicker route for the cyclist
b) The cyclist is going to turn left instead
c) The cyclist thinks The Highway Code does not apply to bicycles
d) The cyclist is slower and more vulnerable

HC rules 163 62

Question: 4.79

Where would you find this road marking?

Mark one answer

a) At a railway crossing
b) At a junction
c) On a motorway
d) On a pedestrian crossing

HC rule 164

Question: 4.80

What do these zigzag lines at pedestrian crossings mean?

Mark one answer

a) No parking at any time
b) Parking allowed only for a short time
c) Slow down to 20 mph
d) Sounding horns is not allowed

HC rule 167

Question: 4.81

Which road user has caused a hazard?

Mark one answer

a) The parked car (arrowed A)
b) The pedestrian waiting to cross (arrowed B)
c) The moving car (arrowed C)
d) The car turning (arrowed D)

HC rules 167 215

Question: 4.82

You are having difficulty finding a parking space in a busy town. You can see there is space on the zigzag lines of a zebra crossing. Can you park there?

Mark one answer

a) No, unless you stay with your car
b) Yes, in order to drop off a passenger
c) Yes, if you do not block people from crossing
d) No, not in any circumstances

HC rule 167

Question: 4.83

You stop for pedestrians waiting to cross at a zebra crossing. They do not start to cross. What should you do?

Mark one answer

a) Be patient and wait
b) Sound your horn
c) Carry on
d) Wave them to cross

HC rules 170 171

Question: 4.84

You are approaching this crossing. You should

Mark one answer

a) prepare to slow down and stop
b) stop and wave the pedestrians across
c) speed up and pass by quickly
d) drive on unless the pedestrians step out

HC rule 171

Question: 4.85

You should never wave people across at pedestrian crossings because

Mark one answer

a) there may be another vehicle coming
b) they may not be looking
c) it is safer for you to carry on
d) they may not be ready to cross

HC rule 171

Question: 4.86

Someone is waiting to cross at a zebra crossing. They are standing on the pavement. You should normally

Mark one answer

a) go on quickly before they step onto the crossing
b) stop before you reach the zigzag lines and let them cross
c) stop, let them cross, wait patiently
d) ignore them as they are still on the pavement

HC rule 171

Question: 4.87

What should the driver of the car approaching the crossing do?

Mark one answer

a) Continue at the same speed
b) Sound the horn
c) Drive through quickly
d) Slow down and get ready to stop

HC rule 171

Question: 4.88

You are approaching a zebra crossing. Pedestrians are waiting to cross. You should

Mark one answer

a) give way to the elderly and infirm only
b) slow down and prepare to stop
c) use your headlights to indicate they can cross
d) wave at them to cross the road

HC rule 171

Question: 4.89

You are driving towards a zebra crossing. Waiting to cross is a person in a wheelchair. You should

Mark one answer

a) continue on your way
b) wave to the person to cross
c) wave to the person to wait
d) be prepared to stop

HC rules 171 183

Question: 4.90

You are approaching a pelican crossing. The amber light is flashing. You must

Mark one answer

a) give way to pedestrians who are crossing
b) encourage pedestrians to cross
c) not move until the green light appears
d) stop even if the crossing is clear

HC rule 172

Question: 4.91

At a pelican crossing, what does a flashing amber light mean?

Mark one answer

a) You must not move off until the lights stop flashing
b) You must give way to pedestrians still on the crossing
c) You can move off, even if pedestrians are still on the crossing
d) You must stop because the lights are about to change to red

HC rule 172

Question: 4.92

At a pelican crossing the flashing amber light means you MUST

Mark one answer

a) stop and wait for the green light
b) stop and wait for the red light
c) give way to pedestrians waiting to cross
d) give way to pedestrians already on the crossing

HC rule 172

Question: 4.93

What must a driver do at a pelican crossing when the amber light is flashing?

Mark one answer

a) Signal the pedestrian to cross
b) Always wait for the green light before proceeding
c) Give way to any pedestrians on the crossing
d) Wait for the red-and-amber light before proceeding

HC rule 172

Question: 4.94

You are waiting at a pelican crossing. The red light changes to flashing amber. This means you must

Mark one answer

a) wait for pedestrians on the crossing to clear
b) move off immediately without any hesitation
c) wait for the green light before moving off
d) get ready and go when the continuous amber light shows

HC rule 172

Question: 4.95

As you approach a pelican crossing the lights change to green. Elderly people are halfway across. You should

Mark one answer

a) wave them to cross as quickly as they can
b) rev your engine to make them hurry
c) flash your lights in case they have not heard you
d) wait because they will take longer to cross

HC rules 174 170 183

Question: 4.96

You have stopped at a pelican crossing. A disabled person is crossing slowly in front of you. The lights have now changed to green. You should

Mark two answers

a) allow the person to cross
b) drive in front of the person
c) drive behind the person
d) sound your horn
e) be patient
f) edge forward slowly

HC rules 174 170 183

Question: 4.97

At puffin crossings which light will not show to a driver?

Mark one answer

a) Flashing amber
b) Red
c) steady amber
d) green

HC rule 175

Question: 4.98

At a puffin crossing what colour follows the green signal?

Mark one answer

a) Steady red
b) Flashing amber
c) Steady amber
d) Flashing green

HC rule 175

Question: 4.99

You are parked in a busy high street. What is the safest way to turn your vehicle around to go the opposite way?

Mark one answer

a) Find a quiet side road to turn round in
b) Drive into a side road and reverse into the main road
c) Get someone to stop the traffic
d) Do a U-turn

HC rule 176

Question: 4.100

You are on a busy main road and find that you are travelling in the wrong direction. What should you do?

Mark one answer

a) Turn into a side road on the right and reverse into the main road
b) Make a U-turn in the main road
c) Make a 'three-point' turn in the main road
d) Turn round in a side road

HC rule 176

Question: 4.101

When may you reverse from a side road into a main road?

Mark one answer

a) Only if both roads are clear of traffic
b) Not at any time
c) At any time
d) Only if the main road is clear of traffic

HC rule 177

Question: 4.102

You want to reverse into a side road. You are not sure that the area behind your car is clear. What should you do?

Mark one answer

a) Look through the rear window only
b) Get out and check
c) Check the mirrors only
d) Carry on, assuming it is clear

HC rule 178

Question: 4.103

You cannot see clearly behind when reversing. What should you do?

Mark one answer

a) Open your window to look behind
b) Open the door and look behind
c) Look in the nearside mirror
d) Ask someone to guide you

HC rule 178

Question: 4.104

Who is especially in danger of not being seen as you reverse your car?

Mark one answer

a) Motorcyclists
b) Car drivers
c) Cyclists
d) Children

HC rule 178

Question: 4.105

You must not reverse

Mark one answer

a) for longer than necessary
b) for more than a car's length
c) into a side road
d) in a built-up area

HC rule 179

5. Road users requiring extra care

Before completing quiz 5 read Highway Code rules 180 - 200.

Question: 5.1

At road junctions which of the following are most vulnerable?

Mark three answers

a) Cyclists
b) Motorcyclists
c) Pedestrians
d) Car drivers
e) Lorry drivers
HC rule 180

Question: 5.2

You are at a road junction, turning into a minor road. There are pedestrians crossing the minor road. You should

Mark one answer

a) stop and wave the pedestrians across
b) sound your horn to let the pedestrians know that you are there
c) give way to the pedestrians who are already crossing
d) carry on; the pedestrians should give way to you
HC rule 182

Question: 5.3

You are turning left into a side road. Pedestrians are crossing the road near the junction. You must

Mark one answer

a) wave them on
b) sound your horn
c) switch on your hazard lights
d) wait for them to cross
HC rule 182

Question: 5.4

You are driving past a line of parked cars. You notice a ball bouncing out into the road ahead. What should you do?

Mark one answer

a) Continue driving at the same speed and sound your horn
b) Continue driving at the same speed and flash your headlights
c) Slow down and be prepared to stop for children
d) Stop and wave the children across to fetch their ball
HC rule 182

Question: 5.5

You are driving in town. There is a bus at the bus stop on the other side of the road. Why should you be careful?

Mark one answer

a) The bus may have broken down
b) Pedestrians may come from behind the bus
c) The bus may move off suddenly
d) The bus may remain stationary
HC rule 182

Question: 5.6

You are turning left from a main road into a side road. People are already crossing the road into which you are turning. You should

Mark one answer

a) continue, as it is your right of way
b) signal to them to continue crossing
c) wait and allow them to cross
d) sound your horn to warn them of your presence
HC rule 182

Question: 5.7
You are turning left at a junction. Pedestrians have started to cross the road. You should

Mark one answer
a) go on, giving them plenty of room
b) stop and wave at them to cross
c) blow your horn and proceed
d) give way to them
HC rule 182

Question: 5.8
What should the driver of the red car (arrowed) do?

Mark one answer
a) Wave the pedestrians who are waiting to cross
b) Wait for the pedestrian in the road to cross
c) Quickly drive behind the pedestrian in the road
d) Tell the pedestrian in the road she should not have crossed
HC rule 182

Question: 5.9
You see a pedestrian with a white stick and red band. This means that the person is
Mark one answer
a) physically disabled
b) deaf only
c) blind only
d) deaf and blind
HC rule 183

Question: 5.10
What action would you take when elderly people are crossing the road?

Mark one answer
a) Wave them across so they know that you have seen them
b) Be patient and allow them to cross in their own time
c) Rev the engine to let them know that you are waiting
d) Tap the horn in case they are hard of hearing
HC rule 183

Question: 5.11
You see two elderly pedestrians about to cross the road ahead. You should
Mark one answer
a) expect them to wait for you to pass
b) speed up to get past them quickly
c) stop and wave them across the road
d) be careful, they may misjudge your speed
HC rule 183

Question: 5.12
You have just passed these warning lights. What hazard would you expect to see next?

Mark one answer
a) A level crossing with no barrier
b) An ambulance station
c) A school crossing patrol
d) An opening bridge
HC rule 184

Question: 5.13
There are flashing amber lights under a school warning sign. What action should you take?
Mark one answer
a) Reduce speed until you are clear of the area
b) Keep up your speed and sound the horn
c) Increase your speed to clear the area quickly
d) Wait at the lights until they change to green
HC rule 184

Question: 5.14
This yellow sign on a vehicle indicates this is

Mark one answer
a) a vehicle broken down
b) a school bus
c) an ice cream van
d) a private ambulance
HC rule 185

Question: 5.15
Where would you see this sign?

Mark one answer
a) Near a school crossing
b) At a playground entrance
c) On a school bus
d) At a 'pedestrians only' area
HC rule 185

Question: 5.16
Where would you see this sign?

Mark one answer
a) In the window of a car taking children to school
b) At the side of the road
c) At playground areas
d) On the rear of a school bus or coach
HC rule 185

Question: 5.17
How will a school crossing patrol signal you to stop?
Mark one answer
a) By pointing to children on the opposite pavement
b) By displaying a red light
c) By displaying a stop sign
d) By giving you an arm signal
HC rule 186

Question: 5.18
What is the main hazard shown in this picture?

Mark one answer
a) Vehicles turning right
b) Vehicles doing U-turns
c) The cyclist crossing the road
d) Parked cars around the corner
HC rule 187

Question: 5.19
You are waiting to come out of a side road. Why should you watch carefully for motorcycles?
Mark one answer
a) Motorcycles are usually faster than cars
b) Police patrols often use motorcycles
c) Motorcycles are small and hard to see
d) Motorcycles have right of way
HC rule 187

Question: 5.20
Motorcyclists are particularly vulnerable
Mark one answer
a) when moving off
b) on dual carriageways
c) when approaching junctions
d) on motorways
HC rule 187

Question: 5.21
Which THREE of the following are hazards motorcyclists present in queues of traffic?
Mark three answers
a) Cutting in just in front of you
b) Riding in single file
c) Passing very close to you
d) Riding with their headlight on dipped beam
e) Filtering between the lanes
HC rule 187

Question: 5.22
You are behind this cyclist. When the traffic lights change, what should you do?

Mark one answer
a) Try to move off before the cyclist
b) Allow the cyclist time and room
c) Turn right but give the cyclist room
d) Tap your horn and drive through first
HC rules 188 154

Question: 5.23
You are approaching this cyclist. You should

Mark one answer
a) overtake before the cyclist gets to the junction
b) flash your headlights at the cyclist
c) slow down and allow the cyclist to turn
d) overtake the cyclist on the left-hand side
HC rule 188

Question: 5.24

There is a slow-moving motorcyclist ahead of you. You are unsure what the rider is going to do. You should

Mark one answer

a) pass on the left

b) pass on the right

c) stay behind

d) move closer

HC rule 188

Question: 5.25

Motorcyclists will often look round over their right shoulder just before turning right. This is because

Mark one answer

a) they need to listen for following traffic

b) motorcycles do not have mirrors

c) looking around helps them balance as they turn

d) they need to check for traffic in their blind area

HC rule 188

Question: 5.26

What is the main hazard you should be aware of when following this cyclist?

Mark one answer

a) The cyclist may move into the left and dismount

b) The cyclist may swerve out into the road

c) The contents of the cyclist's carrier may fall onto the road

d) The cyclist may wish to turn right at the end of the road

HC rule 189

Question: 5.27

The road is wet. Why might a motorcyclist steer round drain covers on a bend?

Mark one answer

a) To avoid puncturing the tyres on the edge of the drain covers

b) To prevent the motorcycle sliding on the metal drain covers

c) To help judge the bend using the drain covers as marker points

d) To avoid splashing pedestrians on the pavement

HC rule 189

Question: 5.28

You are following a motorcyclist on an uneven road. You should

Mark one answer

a) allow less room so you can be seen in their mirrors

b) overtake immediately

c) allow extra room in case they swerve to avoid pot-holes

d) allow the same room as normal because road surfaces do not affect motorcyclists

HC rule 189

Question: 5.29

A person herding sheep asks you to stop. You should

Mark one answer

a) ignore them as they have no authority

b) stop and switch off your engine

c) continue on but drive slowly

d) try and get past quickly

HC rule 190

Question: 5.30

Which THREE should you do when passing sheep on a road?

Mark three answers

a) Allow plenty of room

b) Go very slowly

c) Pass quickly but quietly

d) Be ready to stop

e) Briefly sound your horn

HC rule 190

Question: 5.31

When overtaking a horse and rider you should

Mark one answer

a) sound your horn as a warning

b) go past as quickly as possible

c) flash your headlights as a warning

d) go past slowly and carefully

HC rule 191

Question: 5.32

You notice horse riders in front. What should you do FIRST?

Mark one answer

a) Pull out to the middle of the road

b) Be prepared to slow down

c) Accelerate around them

d) Signal right

HC rule 191

Question: 5.33

You are driving along a country road. A horse and rider are approaching. What should you do?

Mark two answers

a) Increase your speed

b) Sound your horn

c) Flash your headlights

d) Drive slowly past

e) Give plenty of room

f) Rev your engine

HC rule 191

Question: 5.34

How should you overtake horse riders?

Mark one answer

a) Drive up close and overtake as soon as possible

b) Speed is not important but allow plenty of room

c) Use your horn just once to warn them

d) Drive slowly and leave plenty of room

HC rule 191

Question: 5.35

An elderly person's driving ability could be affected because they may be unable to

Mark one answer

a) obtain car insurance

b) understand road signs

c) react very quickly

d) give signals correctly

HC rule 192

Question: 5.36

You are following a car driven by an elderly driver. You should

Mark one answer

a) expect the driver to drive badly

b) flash your lights and overtake

c) be aware that the driver's reactions may not be as fast as yours

d) stay very close behind but be careful

HC rule 192

Question: 5.37

You are following a learner driver who stalls at a junction. You should

Mark one answer

a) be patient as you expect them to make mistakes

b) stay very close behind and flash your headlights

c) start to rev your engine if they take too long to restart

d) immediately steer around them and drive on

HC rule 193

Question: 5.38

How would you react to drivers who appear to be inexperienced?

Mark one answer

a) Sound your horn to warn them of your presence

b) Be patient and prepare for them to react more slowly

c) Flash your headlights to indicate that it is safe for them to proceed

d) Overtake them as soon as possible

HC rule 193

Question: 5.39

When being followed by an ambulance showing a flashing blue beacon you should

Mark one answer

a) pull over as soon as safely possible to let it pass

b) accelerate hard to get away from it

c) maintain your speed and course

d) brake harshly and immediately stop in the road

HC rule 194

Question: 5.40

You are on a dual carriageway. Ahead you see a vehicle with an amber flashing light. What will this be?

Mark one answer

a) An ambulance

b) A fire engine

c) A doctor on call

d) A disabled persons vehicle

HC rule 195

Question: 5.41

Powered vehicles used by disabled people are small and hard to see. How do they give early warning when on a dual carriageway?

Mark one answer

a) They will have a flashing red light

b) They will have a flashing green light

c) They will have a flashing blue light

d) They will have a flashing amber light.

HC rule 195

Question: 5.42

You are following a large articulated vehicle. It is going to turn left into a narrow road. What action should you take?

Mark one answer

a) Move out and overtake on the right

b) Pass on the left as the vehicle moves out

c) Be prepared to stop behind

d) Overtake quickly before the lorry moves out

HC rule 196

Question: 5.43

You are driving along this road. What should you be prepared to do?

Mark one answer

a) Sound your horn and continue

b) Slow down and give way

c) Report the driver to the police

d) Squeeze through the gap

HC rule 196

Question: 5.44
When approaching this bridge you should give way to

Mark one answer
a) bicycles
b) buses
c) motorcycles
d) cars
HC rule 196

Question: 5.45
What type of vehicle could you expect to meet in the middle of the road?

Mark one answer
a) Lorry
b) Bicycle
c) Car
d) Motorcycle
HC rule 196

Question: 5.46
What should you do as you approach this overhead bridge?

Mark one answer
a) Move out to the centre of the road before going through
b) Find another route, this is only for high vehicles
c) Be prepared to give way to large vehicles in the middle of the road
d) Move across to the right hand side before going through
HC rule 196

Question: 5.47
You are following a long vehicle. It approaches a crossroads and signals left, but moves out to the right. You should

Mark one answer
a) get closer in order to pass it quickly
b) stay well back and give it room
c) assume the signal is wrong and it is really turning right
d) overtake as it starts to slow down
HC rule 196

Question: 5.48
You are driving behind a large goods vehicle. It signals left but steers to the right. You should
Mark one answer
a) slow down and let the vehicle turn
b) drive on, keeping to the left
c) overtake on the right of it
d) hold your speed and sound your horn
HC rule 196

Question: 5.49
You are approaching a mini-roundabout. The long vehicle in front is signalling left but positioned over to the right. You should

Mark one answer
a) sound your horn
b) overtake on the left
c) follow the same course as the lorry
d) keep well back
HC rules 196 163

Question: 5.50
What should you do as you approach this lorry?

Mark one answer
a) Slow down and be prepared to wait
b) Make the lorry wait for you
c) Flash your lights at the lorry
d) Move to the right hand side of the road
HC rule 196

Question: 5.51
You are following a long vehicle approaching a crossroads. The driver signals right but moves close to the left-hand kerb. What should you do?

Mark one answer
a) Warn the driver of the wrong signal
b) Wait behind the long vehicle
c) Report the driver to the police
d) Overtake on the right-hand side
HC rule 196

Question: 5.52
You are following this lorry. You should keep well back from it to

Mark one answer
a) give you a good view of the road ahead
b) stop following traffic from rushing through the junction
c) prevent traffic behind you from overtaking
d) allow you to hurry through the traffic lights if they change
HC rule 197

Question: 5.53
Why should you be especially cautious when going past this bus?

Mark two answers
a) There is traffic approaching in the distance
b) The driver may open the door
c) It may suddenly move off
d) People may cross the road in front of it
e) There are bicycles parked on the pavement
HC rule 198

Question: 5.54
You are driving in town. Ahead of you a bus is at a bus stop. Which TWO of the following should you do?
Mark two answers
a) Be prepared to give way if the bus suddenly moves off
b) Continue at the same speed but sound your horn as a warning
c) Watch carefully for the sudden appearance of pedestrians
d) Pass the bus as quickly as you possibly can
HC rule 198

Question: 5.55
A bus is stopped at a bus stop ahead of you. Its right-hand indicator is flashing. You should

Mark one answer
a) flash your headlights and slow down
b) slow down and give way if it is safe to do so
c) sound your horn and keep going
d) slow down and then sound your horn
HC rule 198

Question: 5.56

What is the main hazard the driver of the red car (arrowed) should be most aware of?

Mark one answer

a) Glare from the sun may affect the driver's vision
b) The black car may stop suddenly
c) The bus may move out into the road
d) Oncoming vehicles will assume the driver is turning right
HC rule 198

Question: 5.57

When you approach a bus signalling to move off from a bus stop you should

Mark one answer

a) get past before it moves
b) allow it to pull away, if it is safe to do so
c) flash your headlights as you approach
d) signal left and wave the bus on
HC rule 198

Question: 5.58

You are travelling behind a bus that pulls up at a bus stop. What should you do?

Mark two answers

a) Accelerate past the bus sounding your horn
b) Watch carefully for pedestrians
c) Be ready to give way to the bus
d) Pull in closely behind the bus
HC rule 198

Question: 5.59

As a driver why should you be more careful where trams operate?

Mark one answers

a) Because they do not have a horn
b) Because they do not stop for cars
c) Because they do not have lights
d) Because they cannot steer to avoid you
HC rule 199

Question: 5.60

Ahead of you there is a moving vehicle with a flashing amber beacon. This means it is

Mark one answer

a) slow moving
b) broken down
c) a doctor's car
d) a school crossing patrol
HC rule 200

6. Driving in adverse weather conditions and parking

Before completing quiz 6 read Highway Code rules 201 - 226.

Question: 6.1

You are on a wet motorway with surface spray. You should use

Mark one answer

a) hazard flashers
b) dipped headlights
c) rear fog lights
d) sidelights
HC rules 201 202

Question: 6.2

You should switch your rear fog lights on when visibility drops below

Mark one answer

a) your overall stopping distance
b) ten car lengths
c) 200metres (656feet)
d) 100 metres (328 feet)
HC rule 201

Question: 6.3

You may use front fog lights with headlights ONLY when visibility is reduced to less than

Mark one answer

a) 100 metres (328 feet)
b) 200 metres (656 feet)
c) 300 metres (984 feet)
d) 400 metres (1312 feet)
HC rules 201 211

Question: 6.4

Front fog lights should be used

Mark one answer

a) when visibility is reduced to 100 metres (328 feet)
b) as a warning to oncoming traffic
c) when driving during the hours of darkness
d) in any conditions and at any time
HC rule 201

Question: 6.5

Front fog lights should be used ONLY when

Mark one answer

a) travelling in very light rain
b) visibility is seriously reduced
c) daylight is fading
d) driving after midnight

HC rule 201

Question: 6.6

You may drive with front fog lights switched-on

N 512 CTW

Mark one answer

a) when visibility is less than 100 metres (328 feet)
b) at any time to be noticed
c) instead of headlights on high speed roads
d) when dazzled by the lights of oncoming vehicles

HC rule 201

Question: 6.7

Front fog lights may be used ONLY if

Mark one answer

a) your headlights are not working
b) they are operated with rear fog lights
c) they were fitted by the vehicle manufacturer
d) visibility is seriously reduced

HC rule 201

Question: 6.8

Whilst driving, the fog clears and you can see more clearly. You must remember to

Mark one answer

a) switch off the fog lights
b) reduce your speed
c) switch off the demister
d) close any open windows

HC rules 201 211

Question: 6.9

You are driving in heavy traffic on a wet road. Spray makes it difficult to be seen. You should use your

Mark two answers

a) full beam headlights
b) rear fog lights if visibility is less than 100 metres (328 feet)
c) rear fog lights if visibility is more than 100 metres (328 feet)
d) dipped headlights
e) side lights only

HC rules 201 211

Question: 6.10

You are driving at dusk. You should switch your lights on

Mark two answers

a) even when street lights are not lit
b) so others can see you
c) only when others have done so
d) only when street lights are lit

HC rules 201 95

Question: 6.11

Why are vehicles fitted with rear fog lights?

Mark one answer

a) To be seen when driving at high speed
b) To use if broken down in a dangerous position
c) To make them more visible in thick fog
d) To warn drivers following closely to drop back

HC rules 201 211

Question: 6.12

You are driving through a tunnel and the traffic is flowing normally. What should you do?

Mark one answer

a) Use parking lights
b) Use front spot lights
c) Use dipped headlights
d) Use rear fog lights

HC rule 201

Question: 6.13

You are driving along this motorway. It is raining. When following this lorry you should

Mark two answers

a) allow at least a two-second gap
b) move left and drive on the hard shoulder
c) allow at least a four-second gap
d) be aware of spray reducing your vision
e) move right and stay in the right hand lane

HC rules 202 105

Question: 6.14

You are driving in heavy rain. Your steering suddenly becomes very light. You should

Mark one answer

a) steer towards the side of the road
b) apply gentle acceleration
c) brake firmly to reduce speed
d) ease off the accelerator

HC rule 202

Question: 6.15

You are travelling in very heavy rain. Your overall stopping distance is likely to be

Mark one answer

a) doubled
b) halved
c) up to ten times greater
d) no different

HC rule 202

Question: 6.16

You are following a large lorry on a wet road. Spray makes it difficult to see. You should

Mark one answer

a) drop back until you can see better

b) put your headlights on full beam

c) keep close to the lorry, away from the spray

d) speed up and overtake quickly

HC rule 202

Question: 6.17

You are driving along a wet road. How can you tell if your vehicle is aquaplaning?

Mark one answer

a) The engine will stall

b) The engine noise will increase

c) The steering will feel very heavy

d) The steering will feel very light

HC rule 202

Question: 6.18

You are driving along a wet road. How can you tell if your vehicle's tyres are losing their grip on the surface?

Mark one answer

a) The engine will stall

b) The steering will feel very heavy

c) The engine noise will increase

d) The steering will feel very light

HC rule 202

Question: 6.19

Your overall stopping distance will be much longer when driving

Mark one answer

a) in the rain

b) in fog

c) at night

d) in strong winds

HC rule 202

Question: 6.20

When snow is falling heavily you should

Mark one answer

a) only drive with your hazard lights on

b) not drive unless you have a mobile phone

c) only drive when your journey is short

d) not drive unless it is essential

HC rule 203

Question: 6.21

Before starting a journey in freezing weather you should clear ice and snow from your vehicle's

Mark four answers

a) aerial

b) windows

c) bumper

d) lights

e) mirrors

f) number plates

HC rule 204

Question: 6.22

You are driving on an icy road. What distance should you drive from the car in front?

Mark one answer

a) four times the normal distance

b) six times the normal distance

c) eight times the normal distance

d) ten times the normal distance

HC rule 205

Question: 6.23

Braking distances on ice can be

Mark one answer

a) twice the normal distance

b) five times the normal distance

c) seven times the normal distance

d) ten times the normal distance

HC rule 205

Question: 6.24

Freezing conditions will affect the distance it takes you to come to a stop. You should expect stopping distances to increase by up to

Mark one answer

a) two times

b) three times

c) five times

d) ten times

HC rule 205

Question: 6.25

How can you tell if you are driving on ice?

Mark two answers

a) The tyres make a rumbling noise

b) The tyres make hardly any noise

c) The steering becomes heavier

d) The steering becomes lighter

HC rule 206

Question: 6.26

You are trying to move off on snow. You should use

Mark one answer

a) the lowest gear you can

b) the highest gear you can

c) a high engine speed

d) the handbrake and footbrake together

HC rule 206

Question: 6.27

You are driving on an icy road. How can you avoid wheelspin?

Mark one answer

a) Drive at a slow speed in as high a gear as possible

b) Use the handbrake if the wheels start to slip

c) Brake gently and repeatedly

d) Drive in a low gear at all times

HC rule 206

Question: 6.28
How can you tell when you are driving over black ice?
Mark one answer
a) It is easier to brake
b) The noise from your tyres sounds louder
c) You see black ice on the road
d) Your steering feels light
HC rule 206

Question: 6.29
The roads are icy. You should drive slowly
Mark one answer
a) in the highest gear possible
b) in the lowest gear possible
c) with the handbrake partly on
d) with your left foot on the brake
HC rule 206

Question: 6.30
When driving in falling snow you should
Mark one answer
a) brake firmly and quickly
b) be ready to steer sharply
c) use sidelights only
d) brake gently in plenty of time
HC rule 206

Question: 6.31
You are driving in freezing conditions. What should you do when approaching a sharp bend?
Mark two answers
a) Slow down before you reach the bend
b) Gently apply your handbrake
c) Firmly use your footbrake
d) Coast into the bend
e) Avoid sudden steering movements
HC rule 206

Question: 6.32
Which of these vehicles is LEAST likely to be affected by crosswinds?
Mark one answer
a) Cyclists
b) Motorcyclists
c) High-sided vehicles
d) Cars
HC rule 207

Question: 6.33
Where are you most likely to be affected by a sidewind?
Mark one answer
a) On a narrow country lane
b) On an open stretch of road
c) On a busy stretch of road
d) On a long, straight road
HC rule 207

Question: 6.34
What does this sign mean?

Mark one answer
a) Crosswinds
b) Road noise
c) Airport
d) Adverse camber
HC rule 207

Question: 6.35
You are driving on the motorway in windy conditions. When passing high-sided vehicles you should
Mark one answer
a) increase your speed
b) be wary of a sudden gust
c) drive alongside very closely
d) expect normal conditions
HC rule 207

Question: 6.36
In windy conditions you need to take extra care when
Mark one answer
a) using the brakes
b) making a hill start
c) turning into a narrow road
d) passing pedal cyclists
HC rule 207

Question: 6.37
It is very windy. You are behind a motorcyclist who is overtaking a high-sided vehicle. What should you do?
Mark one answer
a) Overtake the motorcyclist immediately
b) Keep well back
c) Stay level with the motorcyclist
d) Keep close to the motorcyclist
HC rule 208

Question: 6.38
You are about to overtake a slow-moving motorcyclist. Which one of these signs would make you take special care?

Sign A   Sign B
Sign C   Sign D

Mark one answer
a) Sign A
b) Sign B
c) Sign C
d) Sign D
HC rule 208

Question: 6.39
You have to make a journey in foggy conditions. You should
Mark one answer
a) follow other vehicles' tail lights closely
b) avoid using dipped headlights
c) leave plenty of time for your journey
d) keep two seconds behind other vehicles
HC rule 209

Question: 6.40
You are driving in fog. Why should you keep well back from the vehicle in front?
Mark one answer
a) In case it changes direction suddenly
b) In case its fog lights dazzle you
c) In case it stops suddenly
d) In case its brake lights dazzle you
HC rules 209 210

Question: 6.41
Why should you always reduce your speed when travelling in fog?
Mark one answer
a) Because the brakes do not work as well
b) Because you could be dazzled by other people's fog lights
c) Because the engine is colder
d) Because it is more difficult to see events ahead
HC rules 209 210

Question: 6.42
You are following other vehicles in fog with your lights on. How else can you reduce the chances of being involved in an accident?
Mark one answer
a) Keep close to the vehicle in front
b) Use your main beam instead of dipped headlights
c) Keep together with the faster vehicles
d) Reduce your speed and increase the gap
HC rule 210

Question: 6.43
You have to make a journey in fog. What are the TWO most important things you should do before you set out?
Mark two answers
a) Top up the radiator with antifreeze
b) Make sure that you have a warning triangle in the vehicle
c) Check that your lights are working
d) Check the battery
e) Make sure that the windows are clean
HC rules 210 204

Question: 6.44
Why is it dangerous to leave rear fog lights on when they are not needed?
Mark two answers
a) Brake lights are less clear
b) Following drivers can be dazzled
c) Electrical systems could be overloaded
d) Direction indicators may not work properly
e) The battery could fail
HC rule 211

Question: 6.45
You are driving on a clear dry night with your rear fog lights switched on. This may
Mark two answers
a) reduce glare from the road surface
b) make other drivers think you are braking
c) give a better view of the road ahead
d) dazzle following drivers
e) help your indicators to be seen more clearly
HC rule 211

Question: 6.46
You forget to switch off your rear fog lights when the fog has cleared. This may
Mark three answers
a) dazzle other road users
b) reduce battery life
c) cause brake lights to be less clear
d) be breaking the law
e) seriously affect engine power
HC rule 211

Question: 6.47
You have been driving in thick fog which has now cleared. You must switch OFF your rear fog lights because
Mark one answer
a) they use a lot of power from the battery
b) they make your brake lights less clear
c) they will cause dazzle in your rear view mirrors
d) they may not be properly adjusted
HC rule 211

Question: 6.48
Using front fog lights in clear daylight will
Mark one answer
a) flatten the battery
b) dazzle other drivers
c) improve your visibility
d) increase your awareness
HC rule 211

Question: 6.49
While you are driving in fog, it becomes necessary to use front fog lights. You should
Mark one answer
a) only turn them on in heavy traffic conditions
b) remember not to use them on motorways
c) only use them on dual carriageways
d) remember to switch them off as visibility improves
HC rule 211

Question: 6.50

Front fog lights may be used ONLY if

Mark one answer

a) visibility is seriously reduced
b) they are fitted above the bumper
c) they are not as bright as the headlights
d) an audible warning device is used

HC rule 211

Question: 6.51

You have just driven out of fog. Visibility is now good. You MUST

Mark one answer

a) switch off all your fog lights
b) keep your rear fog lights on
c) keep your front fog lights on
d) leave fog lights on in case fog returns

HC rule 211

Question: 6.52

In very hot weather the road surface can get soft. Which TWO of the following will be affected most?

Mark two answers

a) The suspension
b) The grip of the tyres
c) The braking
d) The exhaust

HC rule 212

Question: 6.53

In very hot weather the road surface can get soft. Which TWO of the following will be affected most?

Mark two answers

a) The suspension
b) The steering
c) The braking
d) The exhaust

HC rule 212

Question: 6.54

You are leaving your vehicle parked on a road. When may you leave the engine running?

Mark one answer

a) If you will be parked for less than five minutes
b) If the battery is flat
c) When in a 20 mph zone
d) Never on any occasion

HC rule 214

Question: 6.55

On a clearway you must not stop

Mark one answer

a) at any time
b) when it is busy
c) in the rush hour
d) during daylight hours

HC rule 215

Question: 6.56

You are driving on an urban clearway. You may stop only to

Mark one answer

a) set down and pick up passengers
b) use a mobile telephone
c) ask for directions
d) load or unload goods

HC rule 215

Question: 6.57

When can you park on the left opposite these road markings?

Mark one answer

a) If the line nearest to you is broken
b) When there are no yellow lines
c) To pick up or set down passengers
d) During daylight hours only

HC rule 215

Question: 6.58

What MUST you have to park in a disabled space?

Mark one answer

a) An orange or blue badge
b) A wheelchair
c) An advanced driver certificate
d) A modified vehicle

HC rule 216

Question: 6.59

You are looking for somewhere to park your vehicle. The area is full EXCEPT for spaces marked 'disabled use'. You can

Mark one answer

a) use these spaces when elsewhere is full
b) park if you stay with your vehicle
c) use these spaces, disabled or not
d) not park there unless permitted

HC rule 216

Question: 6.60
In which THREE places would parking cause an obstruction to others?
Mark three answers
a) Near the brow of a hill
b) In a lay-by
c) Where the kerb is raised
d) Where the kerb has been lowered for wheelchairs
e) At or near a bus stop
HC rule 217

Question: 6.61
In which THREE places would parking your vehicle cause danger or obstruction to other road users?
Mark three answers
a) In front of a property entrance
b) At or near a bus stop
c) On your driveway
d) In a marked parking space
e) On the approach to a level crossing
HC rule 217

Question: 6.62
In which THREE places must you NOT park?
Mark three answers
a) Near the brow of a hill
b) At or near a bus stop
c) Where there is no pavement
d) Within 10 metres (32 feet) of a junction
e) On a 40 mph road
HC rule 217

Question: 6.63
What is the nearest you may park to a junction?
Mark one answer
a) 10 metres (32 feet)
b) 12 metres (39 feet)
c) 15 metres (49 feet)
d) 20 metres (66 feet)
HC rule 217

Question: 6.64
In which FOUR places must you NOT park or wait?
Mark four answers
a) On a dual carriageway
b) At a bus stop
c) On the slope of a hill
d) Opposite a traffic island
e) In front of someone else's drive
f) On the brow of a hill
HC rule 217

Question: 6.65
In which TWO places must you NOT park?
Mark two answers
a) Near a school entrance
b) Near a police station
c) In a side road
d) At a bus stop
e) In a one-way street
HC rule 217

Question: 6.66
You are parking on a two way road at night. The speed limit is 40 mph. You should park on the
Mark one answer
a) left with parking lights on
b) left with no lights on
c) right with parking lights on
d) right with dipped headlights on
HC rules 222 223

Question: 6.67
You can park on the right-hand side of a road at night
Mark one answer
a) in a one-way street
b) with your sidelights on
c) more than 10 metres (32 feet) from a junction
d) under a lamp-post
HC rules 222 121

Question: 6.68
You are parked on the road at night. Where must you use parking lights?
Mark one answer
a) Where there are continuous white lines in the middle of the road
b) Where the speed limit exceeds 30 mph
c) Where you are facing oncoming traffic
d) Where you are near a bus stop
HC rules 223 222

Question: 6.69
Your vehicle is parked on the road at night. When must you use sidelights?
Mark one answer
a) Where there are continuous white lines in the middle of the road
b) Where the speed limit exceeds 30 mph
c) Where you are facing oncoming traffic
d) Where you are near a bus stop
HC rule 223

Question: 6.70
You park overnight on a road with a 40 mph speed limit. You should park
Mark one answer
a) facing the traffic
b) with sidelights on
c) with dipped headlights on
d) near a street light
HC rule 223

Question: 6.71
On a foggy day you unavoidably have to park your car on the road. You should
Mark one answer
a) leave your headlights on
b) leave your fog lights on
c) leave your sidelights on
d) leave your hazard lights on
HC rule 225

Question: 6.72
You have to park on the road in fog. You should
Mark one answer
a) leave sidelights on
b) leave dipped headlights and fog lights on
c) leave dipped headlights on
d) leave main beam headlights on
HC rule 225

Question: 6.73
You wish to park facing DOWNHILL. Which TWO of the following should you do?
Mark two answers
a) Turn the steering wheel towards the kerb
b) Park close to the bumper of another car
c) Park with two wheels on the kerb
d) Put the handbrake on firmly
e) Turn the steering wheel away from the kerb
HC rule 226

7. Motorways
Before completing quiz 7 read Highway Code rules 227 - 247.

Question: 7.1
Which FOUR of these must NOT use motorways?
Mark four answers
a) Learner car drivers
b) Motorcycles over 50cc
c) Double deck buses
d) Farm tractors
e) Horse riders
f) Cyclists
HC rule 227

Question: 7.2
Which FOUR of these must NOT use motorways?
Mark four answers
a) Learner car drivers
b) Motorcycles over 50cc
c) Double-decker buses
d) Farm tractors
e) Learner motorcyclists
f) Cyclists
HC rule 227

Question: 7.3
As a provisional licence holder you should not drive a car
Mark one answer
a) over 30 mph
b) at night
c) on the motorway
d) with passengers in rear seats
HC rule 227

Question: 7.4
You are on a motorway. There are red flashing lights above every lane. You must

Mark one answer
a) pull onto the hard shoulder
b) slow down and watch for further signals
c) leave at the next exit
d) stop and wait
HC rule 232

Question: 7.5
You are driving on a road with several lanes. You see these signs above the lanes. What do they mean?

Mark one answer
a) The two right lanes are open
b) The two left lanes are open
c) Traffic in the left lanes should stop
d) Traffic in the right lanes should stop
HC rule 232

Question: 7.6

You are on a motorway. Red flashing lights appear above your lane only. What should you do?

Mark one answer

a) Continue in that lane and look for further information
b) Move into another lane in good time
c) Pull onto the hard shoulder
d) Stop and wait for an instruction to proceed

HC rule 232

Question: 7.7

Immediately after joining a motorway you should normally

Mark one answer

a) try to overtake
b) readjust your mirrors
c) position your vehicle in the centre lane
d) keep in the left lane

HC rule 233

Question: 7.8

When joining a motorway you must always

Mark one answer

a) use the hard shoulder
b) stop at the end of the acceleration lane
c) come to a stop before joining the motorway
d) give way to traffic already on the motorway

HC rule 233

Question: 7.9

You are joining a motorway. Why is it important to make full use of the slip road?

Mark one answer

a) Because there is space available to turn round if you need to
b) To allow you direct access to the overtaking lanes
c) To build up a speed similar to traffic on the motorway
d) Because you can continue on the hard shoulder

HC rule 233

Question: 7.10

What is the national speed limit on motorways for cars and motorcycles?

Mark one answer

a) 30 mph
b) 50 mph
c) 60 mph
d) 70 mph

HC rule 235

Question: 7.11

You are driving on a motorway. By mistake, you go past the exit that you wanted to take. You should

Mark one answer

a) carefully reverse on the hard shoulder
b) carry on to the next exit
c) carefully reverse in the left-hand lane
d) make a U-turn at the next gap in the central reservation

HC rule 237

Question: 7.12

On a three-lane motorway which lane should you normally use?

Mark one answer

a) Left
b) Right
c) Centre
d) Either the right or centre

HC rule 238

Question: 7.13

The left-hand lane on a three-lane motorway is for use by

Mark one answer

a) any vehicle
b) large vehicles only
c) emergency vehicles only
d) slow vehicles only

HC rule 238

Question: 7.14

The left-hand lane of a motorway should be used for

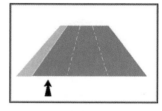

Mark one answer

a) breakdowns and emergencies only
b) overtaking slower traffic in the other lanes
c) slow vehicles only
d) normal driving

HC rule 238

Question: 7.15

What is the right hand lane used for on a three lane motorway?

Mark one answer

a) Emergency vehicles only
b) Overtaking
c) Vehicles towing trailers
d) Coaches only

HC rule 238

Question: 7.16

A basic rule when on motorways is

Mark one answer

a) use the lane that has least traffic
b) keep to the left lane unless overtaking
c) overtake on the side that is clearest
d) try to keep above 50 mph to prevent congestion

HC rule 238

Question: 7.17
For what reason may you use the right-hand lane of a motorway?

Mark one answer
a) For keeping out of the way of lorries
b) For driving at more than 70 mph
c) For turning right
d) For overtaking other vehicles
HC rule 238

Question: 7.18
The right-hand lane of a three-lane motorway is
Mark one answer
a) for lorries only
b) an overtaking lane
c) the right-turn lane
d) an acceleration lane
HC rule 238

Question: 7.19
You are driving at 70 mph on a three-lane motorway. There is no traffic ahead. Which lane should you use?
Mark one answer
a) Any lane
b) Middle lane
c) Right lane
d) Left lane
HC rule 238

Question: 7.20
Which of these IS NOT allowed to travel in the right-hand lane of a three-lane motorway?
Mark one answer
a) A small delivery van
b) A motorcycle
c) A vehicle towing a trailer
d) A motorcycle and side-car
HC rule 239

Question: 7.21
You are on a three lane motorway towing a trailer. You may use the right hand lane when
Mark one answer
a) there are lane closures
b) there is slow moving traffic
c) you can maintain a high speed
d) large vehicles are in the left and centre lanes
HC rule 239

Question: 7.22
On motorways you should never overtake on the left UNLESS
Mark one answer
a) you can see well ahead that the hard shoulder is clear
b) the traffic in the right-hand lane is signalling right
c) you warn drivers behind by signalling left
d) there is a queue of slow moving traffic to your right that is moving slower than you
HC rule 242

Question: 7.23
You are allowed to stop on a motorway when you
Mark one answer
a) need to walk and get fresh air
b) wish to pick up hitch hikers
c) are told to do so by flashing red lights
d) need to use a mobile telephone
HC rule 244

Question: 7.24
When may you stop on a motorway?
Mark three answers
a) If you have to read a map
b) When you are tired and need a rest
c) If red lights show above every lane
d) When told to by the police
e) If your mobile phone rings
f) In an emergency or a breakdown
HC rule 244

Question: 7.25
You are intending to leave the motorway at the next exit. Before you reach the exit you should normally position your vehicle
Mark one answer
a) in the middle lane
b) in the left-hand lane
c) on the hard shoulder
d) in any lane
HC rule 246

8. Breakdowns, accidents, road works, railway level crossings and tramways

Before completing quiz 8 read Highway Code rules 248 - 278.

Question: 8.1
You are on a motorway. When can you use hazard warning lights?

Mark two answers

a) When a vehicle is following too closely
b) When you slow down quickly because of danger ahead
c) When you are towing another vehicle
d) When driving on the hard shoulder
e) When you have broken down on the hard shoulder

HC rules 248 96

Question: 8.2
You have an accident while driving through a tunnel. You are not injured but your vehicle cannot be driven. What should you do first?

Mark one answer

a) Rely on other drivers phoning for the Police
b) Switch off the engine and switch on hazard lights
c) Take the names of witnesses and other drivers
d) Sweep up any debris that is in the road

HC rule 248

Question: 8.3
You are on a motorway at night. You MUST have your headlights switched on unless

Mark one answer

a) there are vehicles close in front of you
b) you are travelling below 50 mph
c) the motorway is lit
d) your vehicle is broken down on the hard shoulder

HC rules 248 249

Question: 8.4
You have broken down on a two way road. You have a warning triangle. It should be displayed

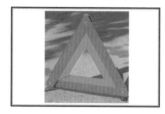

Mark one answer

a) on the roof of your vehicle
b) at least 150 metres (492 feet) behind your vehicle
c) at least 45 metres (147 feet) behind your vehicle
d) just behind your vehicle

HC rule 248

Question: 8.5
You are in an accident on a two way road. You have a warning triangle with you. At what distance before the obstruction should you place the warning triangle?

Mark one answer

a) 25 metres (82 feet)
b) 45 metres (147 feet)
c) 100 metres (328 feet)
d) 150 metres (492 feet)

HC rule 248

Question: 8.6
You have broken down on a two-way road. You have a warning triangle. You should place the warning triangle at least how far from your vehicle?

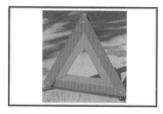

Mark one answer

a) 5 metres (16 feet)
b) 25 metres (82 feet)
c) 45 metres (147 feet)
d) 100 metres (328 feet)

HC rule 248

Question: 8.7
Which of these items should you carry in your vehicle for use in the event of an accident?

Mark three answers

a) Road map
b) Can of petrol
c) Jump leads
d) Fire extinguisher
e) First Aid kit
f) Warning triangle

HC rule 248

Question: 8.8
On the motorway the hard shoulder should be used

Mark one answer

a) to answer a mobile phone
b) when an emergency arises
c) for a short rest when tired
d) to check a road atlas

HC rule 249

Question: 8.9

You have broken down on a motorway. To find the nearest emergency telephone you should always walk

Mark one answer

a) with the traffic flow
b) facing oncoming traffic
c) in the direction shown on the marker posts
d) in the direction of the nearest exit

HC rule 249

Question: 8.10

What should you use the hard shoulder of a motorway for?

Mark one answer

a) Stopping in an emergency
b) Leaving the motorway
c) Stopping when you are tired
d) Joining the motorway

HC rule 249

Question: 8.11

You get a puncture on the motorway. You manage to get your vehicle onto the hard shoulder. You should

Mark one answer

a) change the wheel yourself immediately
b) use the emergency telephone and call for assistance
c) try to wave down another vehicle for help
d) only change the wheel if you have a passenger to help you

HC rule 249

Question: 8.12

Your vehicle has a puncture on a motorway. What should you do?

Mark one answer

a) Drive slowly to the next service area to get assistance
b) Pull up on the hard shoulder. Change the wheel as quickly as possible
c) Pull up on the hard shoulder. Use the emergency phone to get assistance
d) Switch on your hazard lights. Stop in your lane

HC rule 249

Question: 8.13

On a motorway you may ONLY stop on the hard shoulder

Mark one answer

a) in an emergency
b) if you feel tired and need to rest
c) if you accidentally go past the exit that you wanted to take
d) to pick up a hitchhiker

HC rule 249

Question: 8.14

After a breakdown you need to rejoin the main carriageway of a motorway from the hard shoulder. You should

Mark one answer

a) move out onto the carriageway then build up your speed
b) move out onto the carriageway using your hazard lights
c) gain speed on the hard shoulder before moving out onto the carriageway
d) wait on the hard shoulder until someone flashes their headlights at you

HC rule 250

Question: 8.15

Your vehicle has broken down on a motorway. You are not able to stop on the hard shoulder. What should you do ?

Mark one answer

a) Switch on your hazard warning lights
b) Stop following traffic and ask for help
c) Attempt to repair your vehicle quickly
d) Stand behind your vehicle to warn others

HC rule 251

Question: 8.16

You are on a motorway. A large box falls onto the road from a lorry. The lorry does not stop. You should

Mark one answer

a) go to the next emergency telephone and inform the police
b) catch up with the lorry and try to get the driver's attention
c) stop close to the box until the police arrive
d) pull over to the hard shoulder, then remove the box

HC rule 254

Question: 8.17

You are on the motorway. Luggage falls from your vehicle. What should you do?

Mark one answer

a) Stop at the next emergency telephone and contact the police
b) Stop on the motorway and put on hazard lights whilst you pick it up
c) Walk back up the motorway to pick it up
d) Pull up on the hard shoulder and wave traffic down

HC rule 254

Question: 8.18

After an accident, someone is unconscious in their vehicle. When should you call the emergency services?

Mark one answer

a) Only as a last resort
b) As soon as possible
c) After you have woken them up
d) After checking for broken bones

HC rule 257

Question: 8.19

You are the first person to arrive at an accident where people are badly injured. Which THREE should you do?

Mark three answers

a) Switch on your own hazard warning lights
b) Make sure that someone telephones for an ambulance
c) Try and get people who are injured to drink something
d) Move the people who are injured clear of their vehicles
e) Get people who are not injured clear of the scene

HC rule 257

Question: 8.20

An accident has just happened. An injured person is lying in the busy road. What is the FIRST thing you should do to help?

Mark one answer

a) Treat the person for shock
b) Warn other traffic
c) Place them in the recovery position
d) Make sure the injured person is kept warm

HC rule 257

Question: 8.21

You have broken down on a motorway. When you use the emergency telephone you will be asked

Mark three answers

a) for the number on the telephone that you are using
b) for your driving licence details
c) for the name of your vehicle insurance company
d) for details of yourself and your vehicle
e) whether you belong to a motoring organisation

HC rule 257

Question: 8.22

At the scene of an accident you should

Mark one answer

a) not put yourself at risk
b) go to those casualties who are screaming
c) pull everybody out of their vehicles
d) leave vehicle engines switched on

HC rule 257

Question: 8.23

You break down on a motorway. You need to call for help. Why may it be better to use an emergency roadside telephone rather than a mobile phone?

Mark one answer

a) It connects you to a local garage
b) Using a mobile phone will distract other drivers
c) It allows easy location by the emergency services
d) Mobile phones do not work on motorways

HC rule 257

Question: 8.24

At an accident it is important to look after the casualty. When the area is safe, you should

Mark one answer

a) get them out of the vehicle
b) give them a drink
c) give them something to eat
d) keep them in the vehicle

HC rule 257

Question: 8.25

You have stopped at the scene of an accident to give help. Which THREE things should you do?

Mark three answers

a) Keep injured people warm and comfortable
b) Keep injured people calm by talking to them reassuringly
c) Keep injured people on the move by walking them around
d) Give injured people a warm drink
e) Make sure that injured people are not left alone

HC rule 257

Question: 8.26

You arrive at a serious motorcycle accident. The motorcyclist is unconscious and bleeding. Your main priorities should be to

Mark three answers

a) try to stop the bleeding
b) make a list of witnesses
c) check the casualty's breathing
d) take the numbers of the vehicles involved
e) sweep up any loose debris
f) check the casualty's airways

HC rule 257

Question: 8.27

An injured motorcyclist is lying unconscious in the road. You should

Mark one answer

a) remove the safety helmet
b) seek medical assistance
c) move the person off the road
d) remove the leather jacket

HC rule 257

Question: 8.28

You are the first to arrive at the scene of an accident. Which FOUR of these should you do?

Mark four answers

a) Leave as soon as another motorist arrives

b) Switch off the vehicle engine(s)

c) Move uninjured people away from the vehicle(s)

d) Call the emergency services

e) Warn other traffic

HC rule 257

Question: 8.29

Which of the following should you NOT do at the scene of an accident?

Mark one answer

a) Warn other traffic by switching on your hazard warning lights

b) Call the emergency services immediately

c) Offer someone a cigarette to calm them down

d) Ask drivers to switch off their engines

HC rule 257

Question: 8.30

Your vehicle breaks down on the hard shoulder of a motorway. You decide to use your mobile phone to call for help. You should

Mark one answer

a) stand at the rear of the vehicle while making the call

b) try to repair the vehicle yourself

c) get out of the vehicle by the right hand door

d) check your location from the marker posts on the left

HC rule 257

Question: 8.31

You arrive at the scene of a motorcycle accident. No other vehicle is involved. The rider is unconscious, lying in the middle of the road. The first thing you should do is

Mark one answer

a) move the rider out of the road

b) warn other traffic

c) clear the road of debris

d) give the rider reassurance

HC rule 257

Question: 8.32

You arrive at the scene of a motorcycle accident. The rider is injured. When should the helmet be removed?

Mark one answer

a) Only when it is essential

b) Always straight away

c) Only when the motorcyclist asks

d) Always, unless they are in shock

HC rule 257

Question: 8.33

You arrive at an accident. A motorcyclist is unconscious. Your FIRST priority is the casualty's

Mark one answer

a) breathing

b) bleeding

c) broken bones

d) bruising

HC rule 257

Question: 8.34

You have a collision whilst your car is moving. What is the first thing you must do?

Mark one answer

a) Stop only if there are injured people

b) Call the emergency services

c) Stop at the scene of the accident

d) Call your insurance company

HC rule 260

Question: 8.35

You lose control of your car and damage a garden wall. No one is around. What must you do?

Mark one answer

a) Report the accident to the police within 24 hours

b) Go back to tell the house owner the next day

c) Report the accident to your insurance company when you get home

d) Find someone in the area to tell them about it immediately

HC rule 260

Question: 8.36

You are involved in an accident with another vehicle. Someone is injured. Your vehicle is damaged. Which FOUR of the following should you find out?

Mark four answers

a) Whether the driver owns the other vehicle involved

b) The other driver's name, address and telephone number

c) The make and registration number of the other vehicle

d) The occupation of the other driver

e) The details of the other driver's vehicle insurance

f) Whether the other driver is licensed to drive

HC rules 260 261

Question: 8.37

The police may ask you to produce which three of these documents following an accident?

Mark three answers

a) Vehicle registration document

b) Driving licence

c) Theory test certificate

d) Insurance certificate

e) MOT test certificate

f) Road tax disc

HC rule 260

Question: 8.38

A police officer asks to see your documents. You do not have them with you. You may produce them at a police station within

Mark one answer

a) five days

b) seven days

c) 14 days

d) 21 days

HC rule 261

Question: 8.39

At roadworks which of the following can control traffic flow?

Mark three answers

a) A STOP-GO board

b) Flashing amber lights

c) A police officer

d) Flashing red lights

e) Temporary traffic lights

HC rule 262

Question: 8.40

You are entering an area of roadworks. There is a temporary speed limit displayed. You should

Mark one answer

a) not exceed the speed limit
b) obey the limit only during rush hour
c) ignore the displayed limit
d) obey the limit except at night

HC rule 262

Question: 8.41

You are approaching roadworks on a motorway. What should you do?

Mark one answer

a) Speed up to clear the works quickly
b) Always use the hard shoulder
c) Obey all speed limits
d) Stay very close to the vehicle in front

HC rules 262 263

Question: 8.42

You are driving on this dual carriageway. Why may you need to slow down?

Mark one answer

a) There is a broken white line in the centre
b) There are solid white lines either side
c) There are roadworks ahead of you
d) There are no footpaths

HC rules 262 263

Question: 8.43

To avoid an accident when entering a contraflow system, you should

Mark three answers

a) reduce speed in good time
b) switch lanes anytime to make progress
c) choose an appropriate lane early
d) keep the correct separation distance
e) increase speed to pass through quickly
f) follow other motorists closely to avoid long queues

HC rules 262 263 264

Question: 8.44

What does this sign mean?

Mark one answer

a) The right-hand lane ahead is narrow
b) Right-hand lane for buses only
c) Right-hand lane for turning right
d) The right-hand lane is closed

HC rule 263

Question: 8.45

You are in the right hand lane of a dual carriageway. You see signs showing that the right lane is closed 800 yards ahead. You should

Mark one answer

a) keep in that lane until you reach the queue
b) move to the left immediately
c) wait and see which lane is moving faster
d) move to the left in good time

HC rule 263

Question: 8.46

When going through a contraflow system on a motorway you should

Mark one answer

a) ensure that you do not exceed 30 mph
b) keep a good distance from the vehicle ahead
c) switch lanes to keep the traffic flowing
d) stay close to the vehicle ahead to reduce queues

HC rule 264

Question: 8.47
You are on a motorway. There is a contra flow system ahead. What would you expect to find?
Mark one answer
a) Temporary traffic lights
b) Lower speed limits
c) Wider lanes than normal
d) Speed humps
HC rule 264

Question: 8.48
What does this sign mean?

Mark one answer
a) Change to the left lane
b) Leave at the next exit
c) Contraflow system
d) One-way street
HC rule 264

Question: 8.49
You are driving over a level crossing. The warning lights come on and a bell rings. What should you do?
Mark one answer
a) Get everyone out of the vehicle immediately
b) Stop and reverse back to clear the crossing
c) Keep going and clear the crossing
d) Stop immediately and use your hazard warning lights
HC rule 266

Question: 8.50
You are waiting at a level crossing. The red warning lights continue to flash after a train has passed by. What should you do?

Mark one answer
a) Get out and investigate
b) Telephone the signal operator
c) Continue to wait
d) Drive across carefully
HC rule 266

Question: 8.51
You are waiting at a level crossing. A train has passed but the lights keep flashing. You must
Mark one answer
a) carry on waiting
b) phone the signal operator
c) edge over the stop line and look for trains
d) park and investigate
HC rule 266

Question: 8.52
The red lights are flashing. What should you do when approaching this level crossing ?

Mark one answer
a) Go through quickly
b) Go through carefully
c) Stop before the barrier
d) Switch on hazard warning lights
HC rule 266

Question: 8.53
At a railway level crossing the red light signal continues to flash after a train has gone by. What should you do?
Mark one answer
a) Phone the signal operator
b) Alert drivers behind you
c) Wait
d) Proceed with caution
HC rule 266

Question: 8.54
You are driving towards this level crossing. What would be the first warning of an approaching train?

Mark one answer
a) Both half barriers down
b) A steady amber light
c) One half barrier down
d) Twin flashing red lights
HC rule 266

Question: 8.55
Your vehicle has broken down on an automatic railway level crossing. What should you do FIRST?
Mark one answer
a) Get everyone out of the vehicle and clear of the crossing
b) Phone the signal operator so that trains can be stopped
c) Walk along the track to give warning to any approaching trains
d) Try to push the vehicle clear of the crossing as soon as possible
HC rule 272

Question: 8.56
You break down on a level crossing. The lights have not yet begun to flash. Which THREE things should you do?
Mark three answers
a) Telephone the signal operator
b) Leave your vehicle and get everyone clear
c) Walk down the track and signal the next train
d) Move the vehicle if a signal operator tells you to
e) Tell drivers behind what has happened
HC rule 272

Question: 8.57
You have stalled in the middle of a level crossing and cannot restart the engine. The warning bell starts to ring. You should
Mark one answer
a) get out and clear of the crossing
b) run down the track to warn the signal operator
c) carry on trying to restart the engine
d) push the vehicle clear of the crossing
HC rule 272

Question: 8.58
Areas reserved for trams may have
Mark three answers
a) metal studs around them
b) white line markings
c) zig zag markings
d) a different coloured surface
e) yellow hatch markings
f) a different surface texture
HC rule 273

Question: 8.59
Diamond-shaped signs give instructions to

Mark one answer
a) tram drivers
b) bus drivers
c) lorry drivers
d) taxi drivers
HC rule 273

Question: 8.60
On a road where trams operate, which of these vehicles will be most at risk from the tram rails?
Mark one answer
a) Cars
b) Cycles
c) Buses
d) Lorries
HC rule 278

9. Signals and traffic signs part 1
Before completing quiz 9 read Highway Code pages 70 - 73.

Question: 9.1
What does this sign mean?

Mark one answer
a) End of motorway
b) End of restriction
c) Lane ends ahead
d) Free recovery ends
HC page 70

Question: 9.2
You see this amber traffic light ahead. Which light(s) will come on next?

Mark one answer
a) Red alone
b) Red and amber together
c) Green and amber together
d) Green alone
HC page 70

Question: 9.3

You are approaching a red traffic light. The signal will change from red to

Mark one answer

a) red and amber, then green
b) green, then amber
c) amber, then green
d) green and amber, then green
HC page 70

Question: 9.4

These flashing red lights mean STOP. In which THREE of the following places could you find them?

Mark three answers

a) Pelican crossings
b) Lifting bridges
c) Zebra crossings
d) Level crossings
e) Motorway exits
f) Fire stations
HC page 70

Question: 9.5

What does this motorway sign mean?

Mark one answer

a) Change to the lane on your left
b) Leave the motorway at the next exit
c) Change to the opposite carriageway
d) Pull up on the hard shoulder
HC page 70

Question: 9.6

What does this motorway sign mean?

Mark one answer

a) Temporary minimum speed 50 mph
b) No services for 50 miles
c) Obstruction 50 metres (164 feet) ahead
d) Temporary maximum speed 50 mph
HC page 70

Question: 9.7

What does this sign mean?

Mark one answer

a) Through traffic to use left lane
b) Right-hand lane T-junction only
c) Right-hand lane closed ahead
d) 11 tonne weight limit
HC page 70

Question: 9.8

On a motorway this sign means

Mark one answer

a) move over onto the hard shoulder
b) overtaking on the left only
c) leave the motorway at the next exit
d) move to the lane on your left
HC page 70

Question: 9.9

You see this signal overhead on the motorway. What does it mean?

Mark one answer
a) Leave the motorway at the next exit
b) All vehicles use the hard shoulder
c) Sharp bend to the left ahead
d) Stop, all lanes ahead closed
HC page 70

Question: 9.10

At a junction you see this signal. It means

Mark one answer
a) cars must stop
b) trams must stop
c) both trams and cars must stop
d) both trams and cars can continue
HC page 70

Question: 9.11

You are in the right hand lane on a motorway. You see these overhead signs. This means

Mark one answer
a) move to the left and reduce your speed to 50 mph
b) there are roadworks 50 metres (55 yards) ahead
c) use the hard shoulder until you have passed the hazard
d) leave the motorway at the next exit
HC page 70

Question: 9.12

You are travelling along a motorway. You see this sign. You should

Mark one answer
a) leave the motorway at the next exit
b) turn left immediately
c) change lane
d) move onto the hard shoulder
HC page 70

Question: 9.13

You are approaching a zebra crossing where pedestrians are waiting. Which arm signal might you give?

Mark one answer
a) Sign A
b) Sign B
c) Sign C
d) Sign D
HC page 71

Question: 9.14

Which arm signal tells you that the car you are following is going to turn left?

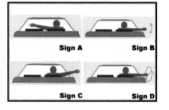

Mark one answer
a) Sign A
b) Sign B
c) Sign C
d) Sign D
HC page 71

Question: 9.15
The driver of this car is giving an arm signal. What are they about to do?

Mark one answer
a) Turn to the right
b) Turn to the left
c) Go straight ahead
d) Let pedestrians cross
HC page 71

Question: 9.16
The driver of the car in front is giving this arm signal. What does it mean?

Mark one answer
a) The driver is slowing down
b) The driver intends to turn right
c) The driver wishes to overtake
d) The driver intends to turn left
HC page 71

Question: 9.17
How should you give an arm signal to turn left?

Mark one answer
a) Sign A
b) Sign B
c) Sign C
d) Sign D
HC page 71

Question: 9.18
You approach a junction. The traffic lights are not working. A police officer gives this signal. You should

Mark one answer
a) turn left only
b) turn right only
c) stop level with the officer's arm
d) stop at the stop line
HC page 72 87

Question: 9.19
What does this signal from a police officer, mean to oncoming traffic?

Mark one answer
a) Go ahead
b) Stop
c) Turn left
d) Turn right
HC page 72 87

Question: 9.20
What is the meaning of this sign?

Mark one answer
a) Local speed limit applies
b) No waiting on the carriageway
c) National speed limit applies
d) No entry to vehicular traffic
HC page 73

Question: 9.21
What does this sign mean?

Mark one answer
a) Bend to the right
b) Road on the right closed
c) No traffic from the right
d) No right turn
HC page 73

Question: 9.22

What does this sign mean?

Mark one answer

a) No overtaking
b) No motor vehicles
c) Clearway (no stopping)
d) Cars and motorcycles only
HC page 73

Question: 9.23

Which of these signs means no motor vehicles?

Mark one answer

a) Sign A
b) Sign B
c) Sign C
d) Sign D
HC page 73

Question: 9.24

What does this sign mean?

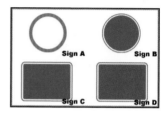

Mark one answer

a) No parking
b) No road markings
c) No through road
d) No entry
HC page 73

Question: 9.25

Which sign means no motor vehicles are allowed?

Mark one answer

a) Sign A
b) Sign B
c) Sign C
d) Sign D
HC page 73

Question: 9.26

Which type of sign tells you NOT to do something?

Mark one answer

a) Sign A
b) Sign B
c) Sign C
d) Sign D
HC page 73

Question: 9.27

Traffic signs giving orders are generally which shape?

Mark one answer

a) Sign A
b) Sign B
c) Sign C
d) Sign D
HC page 73

Question: 9.28
What is the meaning of this sign?

Mark one answer
a) No entry
b) Waiting restrictions
c) National speed limit
d) School crossing patrol
HC page 73

Question: 9.29
Which sign means 'no entry'?

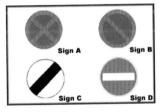

Mark one answer
a) Sign A
b) Sign B
c) Sign C
d) Sign D
HC page 73

Question: 9.30
What does this sign mean?

Mark one answer
a) Roundabout
b) Crossroads
c) No stopping
d) No entry
HC page 73

Question: 9.31
You MUST obey signs giving orders. These signs are mostly in

Mark one answer
a) green rectangles
b) red triangles
c) blue rectangles
d) red circles
HC page 73

Question: 9.32
You see this sign ahead. It means

Mark one answer
a) national speed limit applies
b) waiting restrictions apply
c) no stopping
d) no entry
HC page 73

Question: 9.33
What does this sign mean?

Mark one answer
a) Motorcycles only
b) No cars
c) Cars only
d) No motorcycles
HC page 73

Question: 9.34
This traffic sign means there is

Mark one answer
a) a compulsory maximum speed limit
b) an advisory maximum speed limit
c) a compulsory minimum speed limit
d) an advised separation distance
HC page 73

Question: 9.35
At this junction there is a stop sign with a solid white line on the road surface. Why is there a stop sign here?

Mark one answer
a) Speed on the major road is de-restricted
b) It is a busy junction
c) Visibility along the major road is restricted
d) There are hazard warning lines in the centre of the road
HC page 73 147

Question: 9.36

Which of these signs means that the national speed limit applies?

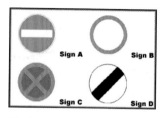

Mark one answer
a) Sign A
b) Sign B
c) Sign C
d) Sign D
HC page 73

Question: 9.37

Which shape is used for a GIVE WAY sign?

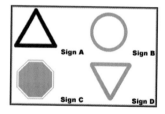

Mark one answer
a) Sign A
b) Sign B
c) Sign C
d) Sign D
HC page 73

Question: 9.38

At a junction you see this sign partly covered by snow. What does it mean?

Mark one answer
a) Cross roads
b) Give way
c) Stop
d) Turn right
HC page 73 147

Question: 9.39

What does this sign mean?

Mark one answer
a) You can park on the days and times shown
b) No parking on the days and times shown
c) No parking at all from Monday to Friday
d) End of the urban clearway restrictions
HC page 73

Question: 9.40

What does this traffic sign mean?

Mark one answer
a) No overtaking allowed
b) Give priority to oncoming traffic
c) Two way traffic
d) One-way traffic only
HC page 73

Question: 9.41

Which type of vehicle does this sign apply to?

Mark one answer
a) Wide vehicles
b) Long vehicles
c) High vehicles
d) Heavy vehicles
HC page 73

Question: 9.42

Which sign means 'no stopping'?

Mark one answer
a) Sign A
b) Sign B
c) Sign C
d) Sign D
HC page 73

Question: 9.43

What does this sign mean?

Mark one answer
a) Waiting restrictions apply
b) Waiting permitted
c) National speed limit applies
d) Clearway (no stopping)
HC page 73

Question: 9.44

Which sign means no overtaking?

Mark one answer
a) Sign A
b) Sign B
c) Sign C
d) Sign D
HC page 73

Question: 9.45

What does this sign mean?

Mark one answer
a) Keep in one lane
b) Give way to oncoming traffic
c) Do not overtake
d) Form two lanes
HC page 73

Question: 9.46

What does this sign mean?

Mark one answer
a) You have priority
b) No motor vehicles
c) Two-way traffic
d) No overtaking
HC page 73

Question: 9.47

Which sign means NO motor vehicles allowed?

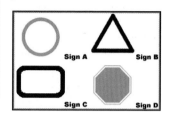

Mark one answer
a) Sign A
b) Sign B
c) Sign C
d) Sign D
HC page 73

Question: 9.48

What shape is a STOP sign at a junction?

Mark one answer
a) Sign A
b) Sign B
c) Sign C
d) Sign D
HC page 73 147

10. Traffic signs part 2 and road/vehicle markings

Before completing quiz 10 read Highway Code pages 74 - 81.

Question: 10.1
What does this sign mean?

Mark one answer
a) Route for trams
b) Give way to trams
c) Route for buses
d) Give way to buses
HC page 74

Question: 10.2
What does this sign mean?

Mark one answer
a) Two-way traffic straight ahead
b) Two-way traffic crossing a one-way street
c) Two-way traffic over a bridge
d) Two-way traffic crosses a two-way road
HC page 74

Question: 10.3
What does this sign mean?

Mark one answer
a) Wait at the barriers
b) Wait at the crossroads
c) Give way to trams
d) Give way to farm vehicles
HC page 74

Question: 10.4
Which of these signs means there is a double bend ahead?

Mark one answer
a) Sign A
b) Sign B
c) Sign C
d) Sign D
HC page 74

Question: 10.5
Which FOUR of these would be indicated by a triangular road sign?

Mark four answers
a) Road narrows
b) Ahead only
c) Low bridge
d) Minimum speed
e) Children crossing
f) T-junction
HC page 74

Question: 10.6
What does this sign mean?

Mark one answer
a) Ring road
b) Mini-roundabout
c) No vehicles
d) Roundabout
HC page 74

Question: 10.7
What does this sign mean?

Mark one answer
a) Crossroads
b) Level crossing with gate
c) Level crossing without gate
d) Ahead only
HC page 74

Question: 10.8
What are triangular signs for?

Mark one answer
a) To give warnings
b) To give information
c) To give orders
d) To give directions
HC page 74

Question: 10.9
What does this sign mean?

Mark one answer
a) With-flow bus and cycle lane
b) Contraflow bus and cycle lane
c) No buses and cycles allowed
d) No waiting for buses and cycles
HC page 74

Question: 10.10
What does this sign mean?

Mark one answer
a) Bus station on the right
b) Contraflow bus lane
c) With-flow bus lane
d) Give way to buses
HC page 74

Question: 10.11
Which sign means 'two-way traffic crosses a one-way road'?

Mark one answer
a) Sign A
b) Sign B
c) Sign C
d) Sign D
HC page 74

Question: 10.12
What does a circular traffic sign with a blue background do?

Mark one answer
a) Give warning of a motorway ahead
b) Give directions to a car park
c) Give motorway information
d) Give an instruction
HC page 74

Question: 10.13
What does this sign mean?

Mark one answer
a) Turn left ahead
b) T-junction
c) No through road
d) Give way
HC page 74

Question: 10.14
What does this sign mean?

Mark one answer
a) Give way to oncoming vehicles
b) Approaching traffic passes you on both sides
c) Turn off at the next available junction
d) Pass either side to get to the same destination
HC page 74

Question: 10.15
What does this sign mean?

Mark one answer
a) Buses turning
b) Ring road
c) Mini roundabout
d) Keep right
HC page 74

Question: 10.16
Which of these signs means turn left ahead ?

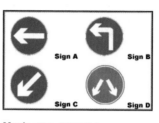

Mark one answer
a) Sign A
b) Sign B
c) Sign C
d) Sign D
HC page 74

Question: 10.17
What does this sign mean?

Mark one answer
a) Service area 30 miles ahead
b) Maximum speed 30 mph
c) Minimum speed 30 mph
d) Lay-by 30 miles ahead
HC page 74

Question: 10.18
What does this sign mean?

Mark one answer
a) Route for trams only
b) Route for buses only
c) Parking for buses only
d) Parking for trams only
HC page 74

Question: 10.19
What does this sign mean?

Mark one answer
a) Adverse camber
b) Steep hill downwards
c) Uneven road
d) Steep hill upwards
HC page 74

Question: 10.20
What does this sign mean?

Mark one answer
a) Minimum speed 30 mph
b) End of maximum speed
c) End of minimum speed
d) Maximum speed 30 mph
HC page 74

Question: 10.21
What does this sign mean?

Mark one answer
a) Contra-flow pedal cycle lane
b) With-flow pedal cycle lane
c) Pedal cycles and buses only
d) No pedal cycles or buses
HC page 74 119

Question: 10.22
What does this sign mean?

Mark one answer
a) No route for pedestrians and
    cyclists
b) A route for pedestrians only
c) A route for cyclists only
d) A route for pedestrians and
    cyclists
HC page 74 119

Question: 10.23
You see this sign ahead. You should
expect the road to

Mark one answer
a) go steeply uphill
b) go steeply downhill
c) bend sharply to the left
d) bend sharply to the right
HC page 74

Question: 10.24
Which of these signs means that you
are entering a one-way street?

Mark one answer
a) Sign A
b) Sign B
c) Sign C
d) Sign D
HC page 74

Question: 10.25
What does this sign mean?

Mark one answer
a) End of dual carriageway
b) Tall bridge
c) Road narrows
d) End of narrow bridge
HC page 74

Question: 10.26
What does this sign mean?

Mark one answer
a) Two-way traffic ahead across a
    one-way street
b) Traffic approaching you has
    priority
c) Two-way traffic straight ahead
d) Motorway contraflow system
    ahead
HC page 74

Question: 10.27
What does this sign mean?

Mark one answer
a) Traffic lights out of order
b) Amber signal out of order
c) Temporary traffic lights ahead
d) New traffic lights ahead
HC page 74

Question: 10.28
Which of these signs means the end of a dual carriageway?

Mark one answer
a) Sign A
b) Sign B
c) Sign C
d) Sign D
HC page 74

Question: 10.29
You should reduce your speed when driving along this road because

Mark one answer
a) there is a staggered junction ahead
b) there is a low bridge ahead
c) there is a change in the road surface
d) the road ahead narrows
HC page 74

Question: 10.30
You see this sign at a crossroads. You should

Mark one answer
a) maintain the same speed
b) carry on with great care
c) find another route
d) telephone the police
HC page 74

Question: 10.31
What does this sign mean?

Mark one answer
a) Cyclists must dismount
b) Cycles are not allowed
c) Cycle route ahead
d) Cycle in single file
HC page 75

Question: 10.32
What does this sign tell you?

Mark one answer
a) No cycling
b) Cycle route ahead
c) Route for cycles only
d) End of cycle route
HC page 75

Question: 10.33
Which sign tells you that pedestrians may be walking in the road as there is no pavement?

Mark one answer
a) Sign A
b) Sign B
c) Sign C
d) Sign D
HC page 75

Question: 10.34
What does this sign mean?

Mark one answer
a) Multi-exit roundabout
b) Risk of ice
c) Six roads converge
d) Place of historical interest
HC page 75

Question: 10.35
What does this sign mean?

Mark one answer
a) Humpback bridge
b) Traffic calming hump
c) Low bridge
d) Uneven road
HC page 75

Question: 10.36
What does this sign mean?

Mark one answer
a) Quayside or river bank
b) Steep hill downwards
c) Uneven road surface
d) Road liable to flooding
HC page 75

Question: 10.37
What does this sign mean?

Mark one answer
a) Level crossing with gate or
   barrier
b) Gated road ahead
c) Level crossing without gate or
   barrier
d) Cattle grid ahead
HC page 75

Question: 10.38
Which sign means that there may be
people walking along the road?

Mark one answer
a) Sign A
b) Sign B
c) Sign C
d) Sign D
HC page 75

Question: 10.39
Which sign means that pedestrians
may be walking along the road?

Mark one answer
a) Sign A
b) Sign B
c) Sign C
d) Sign D
HC page 75

Question: 10.40
Which of these signs warn you of a
pedestrian crossing?

Mark one answer
a) Sign A
b) Sign B
c) Sign C
d) Sign D
HC page 75

Question: 10.41
What does this sign mean?

Mark one answer
a) No footpath ahead
b) Pedestrians only ahead
c) Pedestrian crossing ahead
d) School crossing ahead
HC page 75

Question: 10.42
What does this sign mean?

Mark one answer
a) School crossing patrol
b) No pedestrians allowed
c) Pedestrian zone – no vehicles
d) Pedestrian crossing ahead
HC page 75

Question: 10.43
You are about to overtake when you see this sign. You should

Mark one answer
a) overtake the other driver as quickly as possible
b) move to the right to get a better view
c) switch your headlights on before overtaking
d) hold back until you can see clearly ahead
HC page 75

Question: 10.44
What does this traffic sign mean?

Mark one answer
a) Slippery road ahead
b) Tyres liable to punctures ahead
c) Danger ahead
d) Service area ahead
HC page 75

Question: 10.45
What does this sign mean?

Mark one answer
a) Low bridge ahead
b) Tunnel ahead
c) Ancient monument ahead
d) Accident black spot ahead
HC page 75

Question: 10.46
What does this sign mean?

Mark one answer
a) No trams ahead
b) Oncoming trams
c) Trams crossing ahead
d) Trams only
HC page 75

Question: 10.47
What does '25' mean on this motorway sign?

Mark one answer
a) The distance to the nearest town
b) The route number of the road
c) The number of the next junction
d) The speed limit on the slip road
HC page 76

Question: 10.48
What does this sign mean?

Mark one answer
a) Distance to parking place ahead
b) Distance to public telephone ahead
c) Distance to public house ahead
d) Distance to passing place ahead
HC page 77

Question: 10.49
Which of the following signs informs you that you are coming to a No Through Road ?

Mark one answer
a) Sign A
b) Sign B
c) Sign C
d) Sign D
HC page 77

Question: 10.50
What does this sign tell you?

Mark one answer
a) That it is a no-through road
b) End of traffic calming zone
c) Free parking zone ends
d) No waiting zone ends
HC page 77

Question: 10.51
What does this sign mean?

Mark one answer
a) Hilly road
b) Humps in road
c) Holiday route
d) Hospital route
HC page 77

Question: 10.52
What does this sign mean?

Mark one answer
a) Turn left for parking area
b) No through road on the left
c) No entry for traffic turning left
d) Turn left for ferry terminal
HC page 77

Question: 10.53
What does this sign mean?

Mark one answer
a) T-junction
b) No through road
c) Telephone box ahead
d) Toilet ahead
HC page 77

Question: 10.54
Which sign means 'no through road'?

Mark one answer
a) Sign A
b) Sign B
c) Sign C
d) Sign D
HC page 77

Question: 10.55
What does this sign mean?

Mark one answer
a) No motor vehicles
b) End of motorway
c) No through road
d) End of bus lane
HC page 77

Question: 10.56
What does this sign mean?

Mark one answer
a) End of restricted speed area
b) End of restricted parking area
c) End of clearway
d) End of cycle route
HC page 77

Question: 10.57
What do these motorway signs show?

Mark one answer
a) They are countdown markers to a bridge
b) They are distance markers to the next telephone
c) They are countdown markers to the next exit
d) They warn of a police control ahead
HC page 77

Question: 10.58
What is the meaning of this traffic sign?

Mark one answer
a) End of two-way road
b) Give priority to vehicles coming towards you
c) You have priority over vehicles coming towards you
d) Bus lane ahead
HC page 77

Question: 10.59
Which sign means you have priority over oncoming vehicles?

Mark one answer
a) Sign A
b) Sign B
c) Sign C
d) Sign D
HC page 77

Question: 10.60
This sign means

Mark one answer
a) tourist attraction
b) beware of trains
c) level crossing
d) beware of trams
HC page 77

Question: 10.61
What does a sign with a brown background show?

Mark one answer
a) Tourist directions
b) Primary roads
c) Motorway routes
d) Minor routes
HC page 77

Question: 10.62
What does this sign mean?

Mark one answer
a) No overtaking
b) You are entering a one-way street
c) Two-way traffic ahead
d) You have priority over vehicles from the opposite direction
HC page 77

Question: 10.63
You want to park and you see this sign. On the days and times shown you should

Mark one answer
a) park in a bay and not pay
b) park on yellow lines and pay
c) park on yellow lines and not pay
d) park in a bay and pay
HC page 77

Question: 10.64
This sign is advising you to

Mark one answer
a) follow the route diversion
b) follow the signs to the picnic area
c) give way to pedestrians
d) give way to cyclists
HC page 77

Question: 10.65
You see this sign on the rear of a slow-moving lorry that you want to pass. It is travelling in the middle lane of a three lane motorway. You should

Mark one answer
a) cautiously approach the lorry then pass on either side
b) follow the lorry until you can leave the motorway
c) wait on the hard shoulder until the lorry has stopped
d) approach with care and keep to the left of the lorry
HC page 78

Question: 10.66
Why would this temporary speed limit sign be shown?

Mark one answer
a) To warn of the end of the motorway
b) To warn you of a low bridge
c) To warn you of a junction ahead
d) To warn of road works ahead
HC page 78

Question: 10.67
What might you expect to happen in this situation?

Mark one answer
a) Traffic will move into the right-hand lane
b) Traffic speed will increase
c) Traffic will move into the left-hand lane
d) Traffic will not need to change position
HC page 78 262

Question: 10.68

What does the solid white line at the side of the road indicate?

Mark one answer
a) Traffic lights ahead
b) Edge of the carriageway
c) Footpath on the left
d) Cycle path
HC page 78

Question: 10.69

The white line along the side of the road

Mark one answer
a) shows the edge of the carriageway
b) shows the approach to a hazard
c) means no parking
d) means no overtaking
HC page 78

Question: 10.70

You are on a motorway. You see this sign on a lorry that has stopped in the right-hand lane. You should

Mark one answer
a) move into the right-hand lane
b) stop behind the flashing lights
c) pass the lorry on the left
d) leave the motorway at the next exit
HC page 78

Question: 10.71

You see this line across the road at the entrance to a roundabout. What does it mean?

Mark one answer
a) Give way to traffic from the right
b) Traffic from the left has right of way
c) You have right of way
d) Stop at the line
HC page 78

Question: 10.72

You are driving on a motorway. There is a slow-moving vehicle ahead. On the back you see this sign. You should

Mark one answer
a) pass on the right
b) pass on the left
c) leave at the next exit
d) drive no further
HC page 78

Question: 10.73

'Red routes' in major cities have been introduced to

Mark one answer
a) raise the speed limits
b) help the traffic flow
c) provide better parking
d) allow lorries to load more freely
HC page 79

Question: 10.74

Yellow zig zag lines on the road outside schools mean

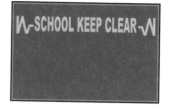

Mark one answer
a) sound your horn to alert other road users
b) stop to allow children to cross
c) you must not wait or park on these lines
d) you must not drive over these lines
HC page 80

Question: 10.75
You should NOT normally stop on these markings near schools

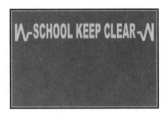

Mark one answer
a) except when picking up children
b) under any circumstances
c) unless there is nowhere else available
d) except to set down children
HC page 80

Question: 10.76
These road markings must be kept clear to allow

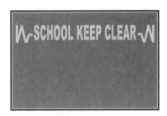

Mark one answer
a) school children to be dropped off
b) for teachers to park
c) school children to be picked up
d) a clear view of the crossing area
HC page 80

Question: 10.77
The road outside this school is marked with yellow zigzag lines. What do these lines mean?

Mark one answer
a) You may park on the lines when dropping off schoolchildren
b) You may park on the lines when picking schoolchildren up
c) You must not wait or park your vehicle here at all
d) You must stay with your vehicle if you park here
HC page 80

Question: 10.78
A tanker is involved in an accident. Which sign would show that the tanker is carrying dangerous goods?

Mark one answer
a) Sign A
b) Sign B
c) Sign C
d) Sign D
HC page 81

Question: 10.79
Where would you expect to see these markers?

Mark two answers
a) On a motorway sign
b) At the entrance to a narrow bridge
c) On a large goods vehicle
d) On a builder's skip placed on the road
HC page 81

11. Annexes

Before completing quiz 11 read Highway Code pages 82 - 93.

Question: 11.1

Motor cars must FIRST have an MOT test certificate when they are

Mark one answer

a) one year old
b) three years old
c) five years old
d) seven years old

HC page 84

Question: 11.2

When is it legal to drive a car over three years old without an MOT certificate?

Mark one answer

a) Up to seven days after the old certificate has run out
b) When driving to an MOT centre to arrange an appointment
c) Just after buying a secondhand car with no MOT
d) When driving to an appointment at an MOT centre

HC page 84

Question: 11.3

Your car needs an MOT certificate. If you drive without one this could invalidate your

Mark one answer

a) vehicle service record
b) insurance
c) road tax disc
d) vehicle registration document

HC page 84

Question: 11.4

An MOT certificate is normally valid for

Mark one answer

a) three years after the date it was issued
b) 10,000 miles
c) one year after the date it was issued
d) 30,000 miles

HC page 84

Question: 11.5

What is the legal minimum insurance cover you must have to drive on public roads?

Mark one answer

a) Third party, fire and theft
b) Fully comprehensive
c) Third party only
d) Personal injury cover

HC page 84

Question: 11.6

Vehicle excise duty is often called 'Road Tax' or 'The Tax Disc'. You must

Mark one answer

a) keep it with your registration document
b) display it clearly on your vehicle
c) keep it concealed safely in your vehicle
d) carry it on you at all times

HC page 85

Question: 11.7

Before driving anyone else's motor vehicle you should make sure that

Mark one answer

a) the vehicle owner has third party insurance cover
b) your own vehicle has insurance cover
c) the vehicle is insured for your use
d) the owner has left the insurance documents in the vehicle

HC page 84

Question: 11.8

Your vehicle needs a current MOT certificate. You do not have one. Until you do have one you will not be able to renew your

Mark one answer

a) driving licence
b) vehicle insurance
c) road tax disc
d) vehicle registration document

HC page 84

Question: 11.9

Which THREE of the following do you need before you can drive legally?

Mark three answers

a) A valid driving licence with signature
b) A valid tax disc displayed on your vehicle
c) A vehicle service record
d) Proper insurance cover
e) Breakdown cover
f) A vehicle handbook

HC page 84

Question: 11.10

Which THREE pieces of information are found on a vehicle registration document?

Mark three answers

a) Registered keeper
b) Make of the vehicle
c) Service history details
d) Date of the MOT
e) Type of insurance cover
f) Engine size

HC page 84

Question: 11.11

You have a duty to contact the licensing authority when

Mark three answers

a) you go abroad on holiday
b) you change your vehicle
c) you change your name
d) your job status is changed
e) your permanent address changes
f) your job involves travelling abroad

HC page 84

Question: 11.12

What is the legal minimum insurance cover you must have to drive on public roads?

Mark one answer

a) Fire and theft
b) Theft only
c) Third party
d) Fire only

HC page 84

Question: 11.13

For which TWO of these must you show your motor insurance certificate?

Mark two answers

a) When you are taking your driving test
b) When buying or selling a vehicle
c) When a police officer asks you for it
d) When you are taxing your vehicle
e) When having an MOT inspection
HC page 85

Question: 11.14

How old must you be to supervise a learner driver?

Mark one answer

a) 18 years old
b) 19 years old
c) 20 years old
d) 21 years old
HC page 85

Question: 11.15

As a provisional licence holder, you must not drive a motor car

Mark two answers

a) at more than 50 mph
b) on your own
c) on the motorway
d) under the age of 18 years of age at night
e) with passengers in the rear seats
HC page 85 227

Question: 11.16

To supervise a learner driver you must

Mark two answers

a) have held a full licence for at least 3 years
b) be at least 21
c) be an approved driving instructor
d) hold an advanced driving certificate
HC page 85

Question: 11.17

A friend wants to teach you to drive a car. They must

Mark one answer

a) be over 21 and have held a full licence for at least two years
b) be over 18 and hold an advanced driver's certificate
c) be over 18 and have fully comprehensive insurance
d) be over 21 and have held a full licence for at least three years
HC page 85

Question: 11.18

To drive on the road learners MUST

Mark one answer

a) have NO penalty points on their licence
b) have taken professional instruction
c) have a signed, valid provisional licence
d) apply for a driving test within 12 months
HC page 84

Question: 11.19

You have just passed your practical test. You do not hold a full licence in another category. Within two years you get six penalty points on your licence. What will you have to do?

Mark two answers

a) Retake only your theory test
b) Retake your theory and practical tests
c) Retake only your practical test
d) Reapply for your full licence immediately
e) Reapply for your provisional licence
HC page 89

Question: 11.20

You have been convicted of driving whilst unfit through drink or drugs. You will find this is likely to cause the cost of one of the following to rise considerably. Which one?

Mark one answer

a) Road fund licence
b) Insurance premiums
c) Vehicle test certificate
d) Driving licence
HC page 89

Question: 11.21

Which FOUR of these MUST be in good working order for your car to be roadworthy?

Mark four answers

a) Temperature gauge
b) Speedometer
c) Windscreen washers
d) Windscreen wiper
e) Oil warning light
f) Horn
HC page 89

Question: 11.22

Which THREE does the law require you to keep in good condition?

Mark three answers

a) Gears
b) Transmission
c) Headlights
d) Windscreen
e) Seat belts
HC page 89

Question: 11.23

While driving, a warning light on your vehicle's instrument panel comes on. You should

Mark one answer

a) continue if the engine sounds alright
b) hope that it is just a temporary electrical fault
c) deal with the problem when there is more time
d) check out the problem quickly and safely
HC page 90

Question: 11.24
Which TWO are badly affected if the tyres are under-inflated?
Mark two answers
a) Braking
b) Steering
c) Changing gear
d) Parking
HC page 90

Question: 11.25
It is illegal to drive with tyres that
Mark one answer
a) have been bought second-hand
b) have a large deep cut in the side wall
c) are of different makes
d) are of different tread patterns
HC page 90

Question: 11.26
The legal minimum depth of tread for car tyres over three quarters of the breadth is
Mark one answer
a) 1 mm
b) 1.6 mm
c) 2.5 mm
d) 4 mm
HC page 90

Question: 11.27
It is essential that tyre pressures are checked regularly. When should this be done?
Mark one answer
a) After any lengthy journey
b) After travelling at high speed
c) When tyres are hot
d) When tyres are cold
HC page 90

Question: 11.28
Excessive or uneven tyre wear can be caused by faults in which THREE?
Mark three answers
a) The gearbox
b) The braking system
c) The accelerator
d) The exhaust system
e) Wheel alignment
f) The suspension
HC page 90

Question: 11.29
Your tyre bursts while you are driving. Which TWO things should you do?
Mark two answers
a) Pull on the handbrake
b) Brake as quickly as possible
c) Pull up slowly at the side of the road
d) Hold the steering wheel firmly to keep control
e) Continue on at a normal speed
HC page 90

Question: 11.30
Excessive or uneven tyre wear can be caused by faults in the
Mark two answers
a) gearbox
b) braking system
c) suspension
d) exhaust system
HC page 90

Question: 11.31
Which TWO things should you do when a front tyre bursts?
Mark two answers
a) Apply the handbrake to stop the vehicle
b) Brake firmly and quickly
c) Let the vehicle roll to a stop
d) Hold the steering wheel lightly
e) Grip the steering wheel firmly
HC page 90

Question: 11.32
Which of these, if allowed to get low, could cause an accident?
Mark one answer
a) Antifreeze level
b) Brake fluid level
c) Battery water level
d) Radiator coolant level
HC page 91

Question: 11.33
Your vehicle pulls to one side when braking. You should
Mark one answer
a) change the tyres around
b) consult your garage as soon as possible
c) pump the pedal when braking
d) use your handbrake at the same time
HC page 91

Question: 11.34
You are testing your suspension. You notice that your vehicle keeps bouncing when you press down on the front wing. What does this mean?
Mark one answer
a) Worn tyres
b) Tyres under-inflated
c) Steering wheel not located centrally
d) Worn shock absorbers
HC page 91

Question: 11.35
Your engine catches fire. What should you do first?
Mark one answer
a) Lift the bonnet and disconnect the battery
b) Lift the bonnet and warn other traffic
c) Call the breakdown service
d) Call the fire brigade
HC page 91

The Highway Code quiz programme

Question: 11.36
What TWO safeguards could you take against fire risk to your vehicle?
Mark two answers
a) Keep water levels above maximum
b) Carry a fire extinguisher
c) Avoid driving with a full tank of petrol
d) Use unleaded petrol
e) Check out any strong smell of petrol
f) Use low octane fuel
HC page 91

Question: 11.37
When leaving your vehicle parked and unattended you should
Mark one answer
a) park near a busy junction
b) park in a housing estate
c) remove the key and lock it
d) leave the left indicator on
HC page 92

Question: 11.38
Which of the following should not be kept in your vehicle?
Mark one answer
a) A first aid kit
b) A road atlas
c) The tax disc
d) The vehicle documents
HC page 92

Question: 11.39
Which of these is most likely to deter the theft of your vehicle?
Mark one answer
a) An immobiliser
b) Tinted windows
c) Locking wheel nuts
d) A sun screen
HC page 92

Question: 11.40
When leaving your car unattended for a few minutes you should
Mark one answer
a) leave the engine running
b) switch the engine off but leave the key in
c) lock it and remove the key
d) park near a traffic warden
HC page 92

Question: 11.41
You are parking your car. You have some valuables which you are unable to take with you. What should you do?
Mark one answer
a) Park near a police station
b) Put them under the drivers seat
c) Lock them out of sight
d) Park in an unlit side road
HC page 92

Question: 11.42
What should you do when leaving your vehicle?
Mark one answer
a) Put valuable documents under the seats
b) Remove all valuables
c) Cover valuables with a blanket
d) Leave the interior light on
HC page 92

Question: 11.43
Which of the following may help to deter a thief from stealing your car?
Mark one answer
a) Always keeping the headlights on
b) Fitting reflective glass windows
c) Always keeping the interior light on
d) Etching the car number on the windows
HC page 92

Question: 11.44
How could you deter theft from your car when leaving it unattended?
Mark one answer
a) Leave valuables in a carrier bag
b) Lock valuables out of sight
c) Put valuables on the seats
d) Leave valuables on the floor
HC page 92

Question: 11.45
You have to leave valuables in your car. It would be safer to
Mark one answer
a) put them in a carrier bag
b) park near a school entrance
c) lock them out of sight
d) park near a bus stop
HC page 92

Question: 11.46
How can you reduce the chances of your car being broken into when leaving it unattended?
Mark one answer
a) Take all contents with you
b) Park near a taxi rank
c) Place any valuables on the floor
d) Park near a fire station
HC page 92

Question: 11.47
When leaving your car to help keep it secure you should
Mark one answer
a) leave the hazard warning lights on
b) lock it and remove the key
c) park on a one way street
d) park in a residential area
HC page 92

Question: 11.48
When parking and leaving your car for a few minutes you should
Mark one answer
a) leave it unlocked
b) lock it and remove the key
c) leave the hazard warning lights on
d) leave the interior light on
HC page 92

Question: 11.49
When parking and leaving your car you should
Mark one answer
a) park under a shady tree
b) remove the tax disc
c) park in a quiet road
d) engage the steering lock
HC page 92

Question: 11.50

You arrive at the scene of an accident. A pedestrian has a severe bleeding wound on their leg, although it is not broken. What should you do?

Mark two answers

a) Dab the wound to stop bleeding
b) Keep both legs flat on the ground
c) Apply firm pressure to the wound
d) Raise the leg to lessen bleeding
e) Fetch them a warm drink

HC page 93

Question: 11.51

At an accident someone is unconscious. Your main priorities should be to

Mark three answers

a) sweep up the broken glass
b) take the names of witnesses
c) count the number of vehicles involved
d) check the airway is clear
e) make sure they are breathing
f) stop any heavy bleeding

HC page 93

Question: 11.52

You arrive at the scene of an accident. It has just happened and someone is injured. Which THREE of the following should be given urgent priority?

Mark three answers

a) Stop any severe bleeding
b) Get them a warm drink
c) Check that their breathing is OK
d) Take numbers of vehicles involved
e) Look for witnesses
f) Clear their airway and keep it open

HC page 93

Question: 11.53

At an accident a casualty has stopped breathing. You should

Mark two answers

a) remove anything that is blocking the mouth
b) keep the head tilted forwards as far as possible
c) raise the legs to help with circulation
d) try to give the casualty something to drink
e) keep the head tilted back as far as possible

HC page 93

Question: 11.54

At an accident a casualty is unconscious but still breathing. You should only move them if

Mark one answer

a) an ambulance is on its way
b) bystanders advise you to
c) there is further danger
d) bystanders will help you to

HC page 92

Question: 11.55

An accident casualty has an injured arm. They can move it freely, but it is bleeding. Why should you get them to keep it in a raised position?

Mark one answer

a) Because it will ease the pain
b) It will help them to be seen more easily
c) To stop them touching other people
d) It will help to reduce the bleeding

HC page 92

Question: 11.56

At an accident a casualty is unconscious. Which THREE of the following should you check urgently?

Mark three answers

a) Circulation
b) Airway
c) Shock
d) Breathing
e) Broken bones

HC page 93

Question: 11.57

You arrive at the scene of an accident. It has just happened and someone is unconscious. Which of the following should be given urgent priority to help them?

Mark three answers

a) Clear the airway and keep it open
b) Try to get them to drink water
c) Check that they are breathing
d) Look for any witnesses
e) Stop any heavy bleeding
f) Take the numbers of vehicles involved

HC page 93

Question: 11.58

You are at the scene of an accident. Someone is suffering from shock. You should

Mark four answers

a) reassure them constantly
b) offer them a cigarette
c) keep them warm
d) avoid moving them if possible
e) loosen any tight clothing
f) give them a warm drink

HC page 92

Question: 11.59

There has been an accident. The driver is suffering from shock. You should

Mark two answers

a) give them a drink
b) reassure them
c) not leave them alone
d) offer them a cigarette
e) ask who caused the accident

HC page 92

Question: 11.60

You are at the scene of an accident. Someone is suffering from shock. You should

Mark three answers

a) offer them a cigarette
b) offer them a warm drink
c) keep them warm
d) loosen any tight clothing
e) reassure them constantly

HC page 92

Question: 11.61
You have to treat someone for shock at the scene of an accident. You should
Mark one answer
a) reassure them constantly
b) walk them around to calm them down
c) give them something cold to drink
d) cool them down as soon as possible
HC page 92

Question: 11.62
When you are giving mouth to mouth you should only stop when
Mark one answer
a) you think the casualty is dead
b) the casualty can breathe without help
c) the casualty has turned blue
d) you think the ambulance is coming
HC page 93

Question: 11.63
You arrive at the scene of an accident. A passenger is bleeding badly from an arm wound. What should you do?
Mark one answer
a) Apply pressure over the wound and keep the arm down
b) Dab the wound
c) Get them a drink
d) Apply pressure over the wound and raise the arm
HC page 93

Question: 11.64
You arrive at the scene of an accident. A pedestrian is bleeding heavily from a leg wound but the leg is not broken. What should you do?
Mark one answer
a) Dab the wound to stop the bleeding
b) Keep both legs flat on the ground
c) Apply firm pressure to the wound
d) Fetch them a warm drink
HC page 93

Question: 11.65
There has been an accident. A motorcyclist is lying injured and unconscious. Why should you usually not attempt to remove their helmet?
Mark one answer
a) Because they may not want you to
b) This could result in more serious injury
c) They will get too cold if you do this
d) Because you could scratch the helmet
HC page 92

Question: 11.66
To start mouth to mouth on a casualty you should
Mark three answers
a) tilt their head forward
b) clear the airway
c) turn them on their side
d) tilt their head back
e) pinch the nostrils together
f) put their arms across their chest
HC page 93

12. Supplementary notes
Before completing quiz 12 read the Highway Code supplementary notes in this book.

Question: 12.1
The Pass Plus scheme has been created for new drivers. What is its' main purpose?
Mark one answer
a) To allow you to drive faster
b) To allow you to carry passengers
c) To improve your basic skills
d) To let you drive on motorways
Supplementary note 1

Question: 12.2
You have third party insurance. What does this cover?
Mark three answers
a) Damage to your own vehicle
b) Damage to your vehicle by fire
c) Injury to another person
d) Damage to someone's property
e) Damage to other vehicles
f) Injury to yourself
Supplementary note 1

Question: 12.3
A newly qualified driver must
Mark one answer
a) display green 'L' plates
b) not exceed 40 mph for 12 months
c) be accompanied on a motorway
d) have valid motor insurance
Supplementary note 1

Question: 12.4
The cost of your insurance may be reduced if you
Mark one answer
a) are under 25 years old
b) do not wear glasses
c) pass the driving test first time
d) take the Pass Plus scheme
Supplementary note 1

Question: 12.5

The cost of your insurance may be reduced if

Mark one answer

a) your car is large and powerful
b) you are using the car for work purposes
c) you have penalty points on your licence
d) you are over 25 years old

Supplementary note 1

Question: 12.6

Your vehicle is insured third party only. This covers

Mark two answers

a) damage to your vehicle
b) damage to other vehicles
c) injury to yourself
d) injury to others
e) all damage and injury

Supplementary note 1

Question: 12.7

Your motor insurance policy has an excess of £100. What does this mean?

Mark one answer

a) The insurance company will pay the first £100 of any claim
b) You will be paid £100 if you do not have an accident
c) Your vehicle is insured for a value of £100 if it is stolen
d) You will have to pay the first £100 of any claim

Supplementary note 1

Question: 12.8

When you apply to renew your vehicle excise licence (tax disc) you must produce

Mark one answer

a) a valid insurance certificate
b) the old tax disc
c) the vehicle handbook
d) a valid driving licence

Supplementary note 1

Question: 12.9

Which age group of drivers is most likely to be involved in a road accident?

Mark one answer

a) 36 to 45-year-olds
b) 55-year-olds and over
c) 46 to 55-year-olds
d) 17 to 25-year-olds

Supplementary note 1

Question: 12.10

You have just passed your test. How can you decrease your risk of accidents on the motorway?

Mark one answer

a) By keeping up with the car in front
b) By never going over 40 mph
c) By staying only in the left hand lane
d) By taking further training

Supplementary note 1

Question: 12.11

A cover note is a document issued before you receive your

Mark one answer

a) driving licence
b) insurance certificate
c) registration document
d) MOT certificate

Supplementary note 1

Question: 12.12

Which of the following may reduce the cost of your insurance?

Mark one answer

a) Having a valid MOT certificate
b) Taking a Pass Plus course
c) Driving a powerful car
d) Having penalty points on your licence

Supplementary note 1

Question: 12.13

Supertrams or Light Rapid Transit (LRT) systems are environmentally friendly because

Mark one answer

a) they use diesel power
b) they use quieter roads
c) they use electric power
d) they do not operate during rush hour

Supplementary note 2

Question: 12.14

How can you, as a driver, help the environment?

Mark three answers

a) By reducing your speed
b) By gentle acceleration
c) By using leaded fuel
d) By driving faster
e) By harsh acceleration
f) By servicing your vehicle properly

Supplementary note 2

Question: 12.15

Motor vehicles can harm the environment. This has resulted in

Mark three answers

a) air pollution
b) damage to buildings
c) reduced health risks
d) improved public transport
e) less use of electrical vehicles
f) using up natural resources

Supplementary note 2

Question: 12.16

To help the environment, you can avoid wasting fuel by

Mark three answers

a) having your vehicle properly serviced
b) making sure your tyres are correctly inflated
c) not over-revving in the lower gears
d) driving at higher speeds where possible
e) keeping an empty roof rack properly fitted
f) servicing your vehicle less regularly

Supplementary note 2

Question: 12.17
Which THREE of the following are most likely to waste fuel?
Mark three answers
a) Reducing your speed
b) Carrying unnecessary weight
c) Using the wrong grade of fuel
d) Under-inflated tyres
e) Using different brands of fuel
f) A fitted, empty roof rack
Supplementary note 2

Question: 12.18
You service your own vehicle. How should you get rid of the old engine oil?
Mark one answer
a) Take it to a local authority site
b) Pour it down a drain
c) Tip it into a hole in the ground
d) Put it into your dustbin
Supplementary note 2

Question: 12.19
On your vehicle, where would you find a catalytic converter ?
Mark one answer
a) In the fuel tank
b) In the air filter
c) On the cooling system
d) On the exhaust system
Supplementary note 2

Question: 12.20
New petrol-engined cars must be fitted with catalytic converters. The reason for this is to
Mark one answer
a) control exhaust noise levels
b) prolong the life of the exhaust system
c) allow the exhaust system to be recycled
d) reduce harmful exhaust emissions
Supplementary note 2

Question: 12.21
Why do MOT tests include a strict exhaust emission test?
Mark one answer
a) To recover the cost of expensive garage equipment
b) To help protect the environment against pollution
c) To discover which fuel supplier is used the most
d) To make sure diesel and petrol engines emit the same fumes
Supplementary note 2

Question: 12.22
To reduce the damage your vehicle causes to the environment you should
Mark three answers
a) use narrow side streets
b) avoid harsh acceleration
c) brake in good time
d) anticipate well ahead
e) use busy routes
Supplementary note 2

Question: 12.23
When a roof rack is not in use it should be removed. Why is this?
Mark one answer
a) It will affect the suspension
b) It is illegal
c) It will affect your braking
d) It will waste fuel
Supplementary note 2

Question: 12.24
How should you dispose of a used battery?
Mark two answers
a) Take it to a local authority site
b) Put it in the dustbin
c) Break it up into pieces
d) Leave it on waste land
e) Take it to a garage
f) Burn it on a fire
Supplementary note 2

Question: 12.25
The pictured vehicle is 'environmentally friendly' because it

Mark three answers
a) reduces noise pollution
b) uses diesel fuel
c) uses electricity
d) uses unleaded fuel
e) reduces parking spaces
f) reduces town traffic
Supplementary note 2

Question: 12.26
Driving at 70 mph uses more fuel than driving at 50 mph by up to
Mark one answer
a) 10%
b) 30%
c) 75%
d) 100%
Supplementary note 2

Question: 12.27
The purpose of a catalytic converter is to reduce
Mark one answer
a) fuel consumption
b) the risk of fire
c) toxic exhaust gases
d) engine wear
Supplementary note 2

Question: 12.28
What is most likely to cause high fuel consumption?
Mark one answer
a) Poor steering control
b) Accelerating around bends
c) Staying in high gears
d) Harsh braking and accelerating
Supplementary note 2

Question: 12.29
A properly serviced vehicle will give
Mark two answers
a) lower insurance premiums
b) you a refund on your road tax
c) better fuel economy
d) cleaner exhaust emissions
Supplementary note 2

Question: 12.30
Catalytic converters are fitted to make the
Mark one answer
a) engine produce more power
b) exhaust system easier to replace
c) engine run quietly
d) exhaust fumes cleaner
Supplementary note 2

Question: 12.31
To reduce the volume of traffic on the roads you could
Mark three answers
a) use public transport more often
b) share a car when possible
c) walk or cycle on short journeys
d) travel by car at all times
e) use a car with a smaller engine
f) drive in a bus lane
Supplementary note 2

Question: 12.32
Which TWO of the following will improve fuel consumption?
Mark two answers
a) Reducing your road speed
b) Planning well ahead
c) Late and harsh braking
d) Driving in lower gears
e) Short journeys with a cold engine
f) Rapid acceleration
Supplementary note 2

Question: 12.33
Which THREE things can you, as a road user, do to help the environment?
Mark three answers
a) Cycle when possible
b) Drive on under-inflated tyres
c) Use the choke for as long as possible on a cold engine
d) Have your vehicle properly tuned and serviced
e) Watch the traffic and plan ahead
f) Brake as late as possible without skidding
Supplementary note 2

Question: 12.34
As a driver you can help reduce pollution levels in town centres by
Mark one answer
a) driving more quickly
b) using leaded fuel
c) walking or cycling
d) driving short journeys
Supplementary note 2

Question: 12.35
A roof rack fitted to your car will
Mark one answer
a) reduce fuel consumption
b) improve the road handling
c) make your car go faster
d) increase fuel consumption
Supplementary note 2

Question: 12.36
As a driver you can cause MORE damage to the environment by
Mark three answers
a) choosing a fuel efficient vehicle
b) making a lot of short journeys
c) driving in as high a gear as possible
d) accelerating as quickly as possible
e) having your vehicle regularly serviced
f) using leaded fuel
Supplementary note 2

Question: 12.37
To help protect the environment you should NOT
Mark one answer
a) remove your roof rack when unloaded
b) use your car for very short journeys
c) walk, cycle, or use public transport
d) empty the boot of unnecessary weight
Supplementary note 2

Question: 12.38
Your vehicle has a catalytic converter. Its purpose is to reduce
Mark one answer
a) exhaust noise
b) fuel consumption
c) exhaust emissions
d) engine noise
Supplementary note 2

Question: 12.39
On which TWO occasions might you inflate your tyres to more than the recommended normal pressure?
Mark two answers
a) When the roads are slippery
b) When driving fast for a long distance
c) When the tyre tread is worn below 2mm
d) When carrying a heavy load
e) When the weather is cold
f) When the vehicle is fitted with anti-lock brakes
Supplementary note 3

Question: 12.40
What can cause heavy steering?
Mark one answer
a) Driving on ice
b) Badly worn brakes
c) Over-inflated tyres
d) Under-inflated tyres
Supplementary note 3

Question: 12.41
Unbalanced wheels on a car may cause
Mark one answer
a) the steering to pull to one side
b) the steering to vibrate
c) the brakes to fail
d) the tyres to deflate
Supplementary note 3

Question: 12.42
You will use more fuel if your tyres are
Mark one answer
a) under-inflated
b) of different makes
c) over-inflated
d) new and hardly used
Supplementary note 3

Question: 12.43
Driving with under-inflated tyres can affect
Mark two answers
a) engine temperature
b) fuel consumption
c) braking
d) oil pressure
Supplementary note 3

Question: 12.44
Turning the steering wheel while your car is stationary can cause damage to the
Mark two answers
a) gearbox
b) engine
c) brakes
d) steering
e) tyres
Supplementary note 5

Question: 12.45
When should you especially check the engine oil level?
Mark one answer
a) Before a long journey
b) When the engine is hot
c) Early in the morning
d) Every 6000 miles
Supplementary note 6

Question: 12.46
You need top up your battery. What level should you fill to?
Mark one answer
a) The top of the battery
b) Half-way up the battery
c) Just below the cell plates
d) Just above the cell plates
Supplementary note 6

Question: 12.47
You have too much oil in your engine. What could this cause?
Mark one answer
a) Low oil pressure
b) Engine overheating
c) Chain wear
d) Oil leaks
Supplementary note 6

Question: 12.48
The fluid level in your battery is low. What should you top it up with?
Mark one answer
a) Battery acid
b) Distilled water
c) Engine oil
d) Engine oil
Supplementary note 6

Question: 12.49
You are driving down a long steep hill. You suddenly notice your brakes are not working as well as normal. What is the usual cause of this?
Mark one answer
a) The brakes overheating
b) Air in the brake fluid
c) Oil on the brakes
d) Badly adjusted brakes
Supplementary note 7

Question: 12.50
The main cause of brake fade is
Mark one answer
a) the brakes overheating
b) air in the brake fluid
c) oil on the brakes
d) the brakes out of adjustment
Supplementary note 7

Question: 12.51
You have been involved in an argument before starting your journey. This has made you feel angry. You should
Mark one answer
a) start to drive, but open a window
b) drive slower than normal and turn your radio on
c) have an alcoholic drink to help you relax before driving
d) calm down before you start to drive
Supplementary note 9

Question: 12.52
Objects hanging from your interior mirror may
Mark two answers
a) restrict your view
b) improve your driving
c) distract your attention
d) help your concentration
Supplementary note 9

Question: 12.53
Why are mirrors often slightly curved (convex)?
Mark one answer
a) They give a wider field of vision
b) They totally cover blind spots
c) They make it easier to judge the speed of following traffic
d) They make following traffic look bigger
Supplementary note 10

Question: 12.54
You are dazzled at night by a vehicle behind you. You should
Mark one answer
a) set your mirror to anti dazzle
b) set your mirror to dazzle the other driver
c) brake sharply to a stop
d) switch your rear lights on and off
Supplementary note 10

Question: 12.55

While driving, this warning light on your dashboard comes on. It means

Mark one answer

a) a fault in the braking system
b) the engine oil is low
c) a rear light has failed
d) your seat belt is not fastened
Supplementary note 11

Question: 12.56

Which instrument panel warning light would show that headlights are on full beam ?

Mark one answer

a) Sign A
b) Sign B
c) Sign C
d) Sign D
Supplementary note 11

Question: 12.57

What does this instrument panel light mean when lit ?

Mark one answer

a) Gear lever in park
b) Gear lever in neutral
c) Handbrake on
d) Handbrake off
Supplementary note 11

Question: 12.58

Anti-lock brakes may not work as effectively if the road surface is

Mark two answers

a) dry
b) loose
c) wet
d) good
e) firm
Supplementary note 12

Question: 12.59

You are driving on a wet road. You have to stop your vehicle in an emergency. You should

Mark one answer

a) apply the handbrake and footbrake together
b) keep both hands on the wheel
c) select reverse gear
d) give an arm signal
Supplementary note 12

Question: 12.60

You arrive at an accident where someone is suffering from severe burns. You should

Mark one answer

a) apply lotions to the injury
b) burst any blisters
c) remove anything stuck to the burns
d) douse the burns with cool liquid
Supplementary note 13

Question: 12.61

You arrive at the scene of an accident. There has been an engine fire and someone's hands and arms have been burnt. You should NOT

Mark one answer

a) douse the burn thoroughly with cool liquid
b) lay the casualty down
c) remove anything sticking to the burn
d) reassure them constantly
Supplementary note 13

Question: 12.62

At an accident you suspect a casualty has back injuries. The area is safe. You should

Mark one answer

a) offer them a drink
b) not move them
c) raise their legs
d) offer them a cigarette
Supplementary note 13

Question: 12.63

At an accident a small child is not breathing. When giving mouth to mouth you should breathe

Mark one answer

a) sharply
b) gently
c) heavily
d) rapidly
Supplementary note 13

Question: 12.64

How can you use the engine of your vehicle to control your speed?

Mark one answer

a) By changing to a lower gear
b) By selecting reverse gear
c) By changing to a higher gear
d) By selecting neutral
Supplementary note 14

Question: 12.65

You will feel the effects of engine braking when you

Mark one answer

a) only use the handbrake
b) only use neutral
c) change to a lower gear
d) change to a higher gear

Supplementary note 14

Question: 12.66

Hills can affect the performance of your vehicle. Which TWO apply when driving up steep hills?

Mark two answers

a) Higher gears will pull better
b) You will slow down sooner
c) Overtaking will be easier
d) The engine will work harder
e) The steering will feel heavier

Supplementary note 14

Question: 12.67

Extra care should be taken when refuelling, because diesel fuel when spilt is

Mark one answer

a) sticky
b) odourless
c) clear
d) slippery

Supplementary note 15

Question: 12.68

To avoid spillage after refuelling, you should make sure that

Mark one answer

a) your tank is only 3/4 full
b) you have used a locking filler cap
c) you check your fuel gauge is working
d) your filler cap is securely fastened

Supplementary note 15

Question: 12.69

You have a loose filler cap on your diesel fuel tank. This will

Mark two answers

a) waste fuel and money
b) make roads slippery for other road users
c) improve your vehicles fuel consumption
d) increase the level of exhaust emissions

Supplementary note 15

Question: 12.70

You may remove your seat belt when carrying out a manoeuvre that involves

Mark one answer

a) reversing
b) a hill start
c) an emergency stop
d) driving slowly

Supplementary note 16

Question: 12.71

When you are NOT sure that it is safe to reverse your vehicle you should

Mark one answer

a) use your horn
b) rev your engine
c) get out and check
d) reverse slowly

Supplementary note 16

Question: 12.72

You are reversing your vehicle into a side road. When would the greatest hazard to passing traffic occur?

Mark one answer

a) After you've completed the manoeuvre
b) Just before you actually begin to manoeuvre
c) After you've entered the side road
d) When the front of your vehicle swings out

Supplementary note 16

Question: 12.73

A heavy load on your roof rack will

Mark one answer

a) improve the road holding
b) reduce the stopping distance
c) make the steering lighter
d) reduce stability

Supplementary note 17

Question: 12.74

What does this sign mean?

Mark one answer

a) Vehicles may not park on the verge or footway
b) Vehicles may park on the left-hand side of the road only
c) Vehicles may park fully on the verge or footway
d) Vehicles may park on the right-hand side of the road only

Supplementary note 18

Question: 12.75

What does this sign mean?

Mark one answer

a) Direction to park and ride car park
b) No parking for buses or coaches
c) Directions to bus and coach park
d) Parking area for cars and coaches

Supplementary note 18

Question: 12.76

You are going through a tunnel and you see this sign. What does it mean?

Mark one answer

a) Direction to emergency pedestrian exit
b) Beware of pedestrians, no footpath ahead
c) No access for pedestrians
d) Beware of pedestrians crossing ahead

Supplementary note 18

Question: 12.77

Which is the sign for a ring road?

Mark one answer

a) Sign A
b) Sign B
c) Sign C
d) Sign D

Supplementary note 18

Question: 12.78

What does this sign mean?

Mark one answer

a) Route for lorries
b) Ring road
c) Rest area
d) Roundabout

Supplementary note 18

Question: 12.79

What do these road markings outside a school mean?

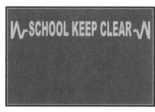

Mark one answer

a) You may park here if you are a teacher
b) Sound your horn before parking
c) When parking use your hazard warning lights
d) You must not wait or park your vehicle here

Supplementary note 18

Question: 12.80

What is the reason for the area marked in red and white along the centre of this road?

Mark one answer

a) It is to separate traffic flowing in opposite directions
b) It marks an area to be used by overtaking motorcyclists
c) It is a temporary marking to warn of the roadworks
d) It is separating the two sides of the dual carriageway

Supplementary note 18

Question: 12.81

Why are these yellow lines painted across the road?

Mark one answer

a) To help you choose the correct lane
b) To help you keep the correct separation distance
c) To make you aware of your speed
d) To tell you the distance to the roundabout

Supplementary note 18

Question: 12.82

When driving through a tunnel you should

Mark one answer

a) Look out for variable message signs
b) Use your air conditioning system
c) Switch on your rear fog lights
d) Always use your windscreen wipers

Supplementary note 18

Question: 12.83

You are going through a tunnel. What systems are provided to warn of any accidents or congestion?

Mark one answer

a) Double white centre lines
b) Variable message signs
c) Chevron 'distance markers'
d) Rumble strips

Supplementary note 18

Question: 12.84

You must not stop on these road markings because you may obstruct

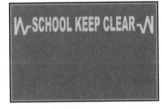

Mark one answer

a) childrens view of the crossing area
b) teachers access to the school
c) delivery vehicles access to the school
d) emergency vehicles access to the school

Supplementary note 18

Question: 12.85

You will see these markers when approaching

Mark one answer

a) the end of a motorway
b) a concealed level crossing
c) a concealed speed limit sign
d) the end of a dual carriageway

Supplementary note 18

Question: 12.86

A rumble device is designed to

Mark two answers

a) give directions
b) prevent cattle escaping
c) alert you to low tyre pressure
d) alert you to a hazard
e) encourage you to reduce speed

Supplementary note 18

Question: 12.87

You are going through a tunnel. What should you look out for that warns of accidents or congestion?

Mark one answer

a) Hazard warning lines
b) Other drivers flashing their lights
c) Variable message signs
d) Areas marked with hatch markings

Supplementary note 18

Question: 12.88

You see these markings on the road. Why are they there?

Mark one answer

a) To show a safe distance between vehicles
b) To keep the area clear of traffic
c) To make you aware of your speed
d) To warn you to change direction

Supplementary note 18

Question: 12.89

You are approaching a busy junction. There are several lanes with road markings. At the last moment you realise that you are in the wrong lane. You should

Mark one answer

a) continue in that lane
b) force your way across
c) stop until the area has cleared
d) use clear arm signals to cut across

Supplementary note 19

Question: 12.90

You take the wrong route and find you are on a one-way street. You should

Mark one answer

a) reverse out of the road
b) turn round in a side road
c) continue to the end of the road
d) reverse into a driveway

Supplementary note 19

Question: 12.91

You are towing a caravan. Which is the safest type of rear view mirror to use?

Mark one answer

a) Interior wide-angle-view mirror
b) Extended-arm side mirrors
c) Ordinary door mirrors
d) Ordinary interior mirror

Supplementary note 20

Question: 12.92

Are passengers allowed to ride in a caravan that is being towed?

Mark one answer

a) Yes if they are over fourteen
b) No not at any time
c) Only if all the seats in the towing vehicle are full
d) Only if a stabilizer is fitted

Supplementary note 20

Question: 12.93

A trailer must stay securely hitched-up to the towing vehicle. What additional safety device can be fitted to the trailer braking system?

Mark one answer

a) Stabiliser
b) Jockey wheel
c) Corner steadies
d) Breakaway cable

Supplementary note 20

Question: 12.94

You are planning to tow a caravan. Which of these will mostly help to aid the vehicle handling?

Mark one answer

a) A jockey-wheel fitted to the towbar
b) Power steering fitted to the towing vehicle
c) Anti-lock brakes fitted to the towing vehicle
d) A stabiliser fitted to the towbar

Supplementary note 20

Question: 12.95

When driving a car fitted with automatic transmission what would you use 'kick down' for?

Mark one answer

a) Cruise control
b) Quick acceleration
c) Slow braking
d) Fuel economy

Supplementary note 21

Question: 12.96

The MAIN benefit of having four-wheel drive is to improve

Mark one answer

a) road holding
b) fuel consumption
c) stopping distances
d) passenger comfort

Supplementary note 22

Question: 12.97

What type of emergency vehicle is fitted with a green flashing beacon?

Mark one answer

a) Fire engine
b) Road gritter
c) Ambulance
d) Doctor's car

Supplementary note 23

Question: 12.98

A vehicle has a flashing green beacon. What does this mean?

Mark one answer

a) A doctor is answering an emergency call
b) The vehicle is slow-moving
c) It is a motorway police patrol vehicle
d) A vehicle is carrying hazardous chemicals

Supplementary note 23

Question: 12.99

Which of the following vehicles will use blue flashing beacons?

Mark three answers

a) Motorway maintenance
b) Bomb disposal
c) Blood transfusion
d) Police patrol
e) Breakdown recovery

Supplementary note 23

Question: 12.100

A flashing green beacon on a vehicle means

Mark one answer

a) police on non-urgent duties
b) doctor on an emergency call
c) road safety patrol operating
d) gritting in progress

Supplementary note 23

Question: 12.101

Which THREE of these emergency services might have blue flashing beacons?

Mark three answers

a) Coastguard
b) Bomb disposal
c) Gritting lorries
d) Animal ambulances
e) Mountain rescue
f) Doctors' cars

Supplementary note 23

Question: 12.102

Windscreen pillars can obstruct your view. You should take particular care when

Mark one answer

a) driving on a motorway
b) driving on a dual carriageway
c) approaching a one-way street
d) approaching bends and junctions

Supplementary note 24

Question: 12.103

You want to turn right from a junction but your view is restricted by parked vehicles. What should you do?

Mark one answer

a) Move out quickly, but be prepared to stop
b) Sound your horn and pull out if there is no reply
c) Stop, then move slowly forward until you have a clear view
d) Stop, get out and look along the main road to check

Supplementary note 24

Question: 12.104
You want to turn left at this junction. The view of the main road is restricted. What should you do?

Mark one answer
a) Stay well back and wait to see if something comes
b) Build up your speed so that you can emerge quickly
c) Stop and apply the handbrake even if the road is clear
d) Approach slowly and edge out until you can see more clearly
Supplementary note 24

Question: 12.105
You are waiting to emerge from a junction. The screen pillar is restricting your view. What should you be particularly aware of?

Mark one answer
a) Lorries
b) Buses
c) Motorcyclists
d) Coaches
Supplementary note 24

Question: 12.106
Why must you take extra care when turning right at this junction?

Mark one answer
a) Road surface is poor
b) Footpaths are narrow
c) Road markings are faint
d) There is reduced visibility
Supplementary note 24

Question: 12.107
You are driving in busy traffic. You want to pull up on the left just after a junction on the left. When should you signal?

Mark one answer
a) As you are passing or just after the junction
b) Just before you reach the junction
c) Well before you reach the junction
d) It would be better not to signal at all
Supplementary note 24

Question: 12.108
You are approaching unmarked crossroads. How should you deal with this type of junction?

Mark one answer
a) Accelerate and keep to the middle
b) Slow down and keep to the right
c) Accelerate looking to the left
d) Slow down and look both ways
Supplementary note 24

Question: 12.109
You are waiting to emerge left from a minor road. A large vehicle is approaching from the right. You have time to turn, but you should wait. Why?

Mark one answer
a) The large vehicle can easily hide an overtaking vehicle
b) The large vehicle can turn suddenly
c) The large vehicle is difficult to steer in a straight line
d) The large vehicle can easily hide vehicles from the left
Supplementary note 24

Question: 12.110
You are approaching crossroads. The traffic lights have failed. What should you do?

Mark one answer
a) Brake and stop only for large vehicles
b) Brake sharply to a stop before looking
c) Be prepared to brake sharply to a stop
d) Be prepared to stop for any traffic.
Supplementary note 24

Question: 12.111
When emerging from junctions which is most likely to obstruct your view?

Mark one answer
a) Windscreen pillars
b) Steering wheel
c) Interior mirror
d) Windscreen wipers
Supplementary note 24

Question: 12.112
You are driving in slow-moving queues of traffic. Just before changing lane you should

Mark one answer
a) sound the horn
b) look for motorcyclists filtering through the traffic
c) give a 'slowing down' arm signal
d) change down to first gear
Supplementary note 25

Question: 12.113

You are in a line of traffic. The driver behind you is following very closely. What action should you take?

Mark one answer

a) Ignore the following driver and continue to drive within the speed limit
b) Slow down, gradually increasing the gap between you and the vehicle in front
c) Signal left and wave the following driver past
d) Move over to a position just left of the centre line of the road

Supplementary note 26

Question: 12.114

'Tailgating' means

Mark one answer

a) using the rear door of a hatchback car
b) reversing into a parking space
c) following another vehicle too closely
d) driving with rear fog lights on

Supplementary note 26

Question: 12.115

You are on a road which has speed humps. A driver in front is travelling slower than you. You should

Mark one answer

a) sound your horn
b) overtake as soon as you can
c) flash your headlights
d) slow down and stay behind

Supplementary note 26

Question: 12.116

In heavy motorway traffic you are being followed closely by the vehicle behind. How can you lower the risk of an accident?

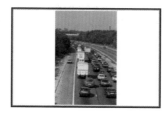

Mark one answer

a) Increase your distance from the vehicle in front
b) Tap your foot on the brake pedal sharply
c) Switch on your hazard lights
d) Move onto the hard shoulder and stop

Supplementary note 26

Question: 12.117

When following a large vehicle you should keep well back because

Mark one answer

a) it allows you to corner more quickly
b) it helps the large vehicle to stop more easily
c) it allows the driver to see you in the mirrors
d) it helps you to keep out of the wind

Supplementary note 26

Question: 12.118

In which of these situations should you avoid overtaking?

Mark one answer

a) Just after a bend
b) In a one-way street
c) On a 30 mph road
d) Approaching a dip in the road

Supplementary note 27

Question: 12.119

As you approach this bridge you should

Mark three answers

a) move into the middle of the road to get a better view
b) slow down
c) get over the bridge as quickly as possible
d) consider using your horn
e) find another route
f) beware of pedestrians

Supplementary note 28

Question: 12.120

You are driving downhill. There is a car parked on the other side of the road. Large, slow lorries are coming towards you. You should

Mark one answer

a) keep going because you have the right of way
b) slow down and give way
c) speed up and get past quickly
d) pull over on the right behind the parked car

Supplementary note 29

Question: 12.121

When driving in fog, which of the following are correct?

Mark three answers

a) Use dipped headlights
b) Use headlights on full beam
c) Allow more time for your journey
d) Keep close to the car in front
e) Slow down
f) Use side lights only

Supplementary note 30

Question: 12.122
Using rear fog lights in clear daylight will
Mark one answer
a) be useful when towing a trailer
b) give extra protection
c) dazzle other drivers
d) make following drivers keep back
Supplementary note 30

Question: 12.123
Chains can be fitted to your wheels to help prevent
Mark one answer
a) damage to the road surface
b) wear to the tyres
c) skidding in deep snow
d) the brakes locking
Supplementary note 30

Question: 12.124
Where is the safest place to park your vehicle at night?
Mark one answer
a) In a garage
b) On a busy road
c) In a quiet car park
d) Near a red route
Supplementary note 31

Question: 12.125
Wherever possible, which one of the following should you do when parking at night?
Mark one answer
a) Park in a quiet car park
b) Park in a well lit area
c) Park facing against the flow of traffic
d) Park next to a busy junction
Supplementary note 31

Question: 12.126
How can you help to prevent your car radio being stolen?
Mark one answer
a) Park in an unlit area
b) Hide the radio with a blanket
c) Park near a busy junction
d) Install a security coded radio
Supplementary note 31

Question: 12.127
You are away from home and have to park your vehicle overnight. Where should you leave it?
Mark one answer
a) Opposite another parked vehicle
b) In a quiet road
c) Opposite a traffic island
d) In a secure car park
Supplementary note 31

Question: 12.128
To help keep your car secure you could join a
Mark one answer
a) vehicle breakdown organisation
b) vehicle watch scheme
c) advanced drivers scheme
d) car maintenance class
Supplementary note 31

Question: 12.129
To help keep your vehicle secure at night where should you park?
Mark one answer
a) Near a police station
b) In a quiet road
c) On a red route
d) In a well lit area
Supplementary note 31

Question: 12.130
When leaving your vehicle where should you park if possible?
Mark one answer
a) Opposite a traffic island
b) In a secure car park
c) On a bend
d) At or near a taxi rank
Supplementary note 31

Question: 12.131
How can you lessen the risk of your vehicle being broken into at night?
Mark one answer
a) Leave it in a well lit area
b) Park in a quiet side road
c) Don't engage the steering lock
d) Park in a poorly lit area
Supplementary note 31

Question: 12.132
Which of the following types of crossing can detect when people are on them?
Mark one answer
a) Pelican
b) Toucan
c) Zebra
d) Puffin
Supplementary note 32

Question: 12.133
You are approaching a red light at a puffin crossing. Pedestrians are on the crossing. The red light will stay on until
Mark one answer
a) you start to edge forward on to the crossing
b) the pedestrians have reached a safe position
c) the pedestrians are clear of the front of your vehicle
d) a driver from the opposite direction reaches the crossing
Supplementary note 32

Question: 12.134
You are approaching traffic lights that have been on green for some time. You should
Mark one answer
a) accelerate hard
b) maintain your speed
c) be ready to stop
d) brake hard
Supplementary note 32

Question: 12.135
You see a pedestrian with a dog. The dog has a bright orange lead and collar. This especially warns you that the pedestrian is
Mark one answer
a) elderly
b) dog training
c) colour blind
d) deaf
Supplementary note 32

Question: 12.136

Which TWO of the following are correct? When overtaking at night you should

Mark two answers

a) WAIT until a bend so that you can see the oncoming headlights
b) sound your horn twice before moving out
c) be careful because you can see less
d) beware of bends in the road ahead
e) put headlights on full beam

Supplementary note 33

Question: 12.137

You are waiting in a traffic queue at night. To avoid dazzling following drivers you should

Mark one answer

a) apply the handbrake only
b) apply the footbrake only
c) switch off your headlights
d) use both the handbrake and footbrake

Supplementary note 33

Question: 12.138

You are driving at night with full beam headlights on. A vehicle is overtaking you. You should dip your lights

Mark one answer

a) some time after the vehicle has passed you
b) before the vehicle starts to pass you
c) only if the other driver dips their headlights
d) as soon as the vehicle passes you

Supplementary note 33

Question: 12.139

You are travelling along the left lane of a three lane motorway. Traffic is joining from a slip road. You should

Mark one answer

a) race the other vehicles
b) move to another lane
c) maintain a steady speed
d) switch on your hazard flashers

Supplementary note 34

Question: 12.140

Why is it particularly important to carry out a check on your vehicle before making a long motorway journey?

Mark one answer

a) You will have to do more harsh braking on motorways
b) Motorway service stations do not deal with breakdowns
c) The road surface will wear down the tyres faster
d) Continuous high speeds may increase the risk of your vehicle breaking down

Supplementary note 34

Question: 12.141

Where would you see these road markings?

Mark one answer

a) At a level crossing
b) On a motorway slip road
c) At a pedestrian crossing
d) On a single-track road

Supplementary note 34

Question: 12.142

You see a car on the hard shoulder of a motorway with a HELP pennant displayed. This means the driver is most likely to be

Mark one answer

a) a disabled person
b) first aid trained
c) a foreign visitor
d) a rescue patrol person

Supplementary note 34

Question: 12.143

How should you use the emergency telephone on a motorway?

Mark one answer

a) Stay close to the carriageway
b) Face the oncoming traffic
c) Keep your back to the traffic
d) Stand on the hard shoulder

Supplementary note 34

Question: 12.144

The emergency telephones on a motorway are connected to the

Mark one answer

a) ambulance service
b) police control
c) fire brigade
d) breakdown service

Supplementary note 34

Answers Section: 1

Book No		DSA No
1.1	b	6.34
1.2	ad	6.8
1.3	a	6.42
1.4	d	10.25
1.5	d	6.7
1.6	a	2.21
1.7	bd	10.26
1.8	a	6.24
1.9	d	6.25
1.10	b	3.33
1.11	b	3.32
1.12	d	3.34
1.13	a	14.4
1.14	a	14.2
1.15	a	14.9
1.16	a	14.12
1.17	bc	14.11
1.18	d	14.5
1.19	c	14.14
1.20	d	3.36
1.21	b	3.41
1.22	c	3.35
1.23	a	14.13
1.24	a	3.70
1.25	d	5.52
1.26	abe	12.21
1.27	cd	5.58
1.28	a	5.87
1.29	b	5.81
1.30	ac	5.59
1.31	abe	5.86
1.32	d	5.72
1.33	cd	5.83
1.34	abc	5.65
1.35	a	5.64
1.36	b	5.63
1.37	b	5.23
1.38	a	5.62
1.39	ad	1.13
1.40	ab	5.60
1.41	be	9.10
1.42	b	5.82
1.43	d	5.75
1.44	d	13.64
1.45	b	13.62
1.46	d	5.84
1.47	c	5.66
1.48	abd	5.76
1.49	ace	5.85
1.50	abc	5.77
1.51	c	5.55
1.52	b	5.53
1.53	d	5.78
1.54	c	5.57
1.55	d	5.56
1.56	c	5.67
1.57	c	5.79
1.58	a	5.61
1.59	ab	5.80

Answers Section: 2

Book No		DSA No
2.1	a	10.75
2.2	b	4.8
2.3	b	11.126
2.4	b	11.155
2.5	d	5.8
2.6	b	11.151
2.7	ace	10.22
2.8	abc	10.70
2.9	b	11.104
2.10	a	11.103
2.11	c	11.145
2.12	d	2.24
2.13	d	2.23
2.14	c	3.5
2.15	c	11.133
2.16	d	3.14
2.17	a	11.134
2.18	a	2.18
2.19	c	5.70
2.20	c	2.29
2.21	d	8.55
2.22	b	8.54
2.23	c	8.59
2.24	b	8.36
2.25	d	10.29
2.26	d	8.15
2.27	b	2.34
2.28	c	8.20
2.29	b	8.32
2.30	a	9.36
2.31	d	13.66
2.32	a	5.91
2.33	d	5.92
2.34	a	5.93
2.35	ab	13.36
2.36	b	11.152
2.37	c	9.48
2.38	a	13.37
2.39	a	5.88
2.40	d	5.89
2.41	a	13.65
2.42	c	4.18
2.43	b	4.19
2.44	b	4.14
2.45	c	8.25
2.46	b	4.16
2.47	b	4.31
2.48	bc	4.42
2.49	d	4.41
2.50	c	4.32
2.51	b	4.30
2.52	d	3.29
2.53	b	4.34
2.54	c	4.33
2.55	b	4.43
2.56	b	4.35
2.57	c	4.37
2.58	c	4.38
2.59	b	4.39
2.60	c	4.40
2.61	d	4.54
2.62	d	4.45
2.63	b	4.12
2.64	d	11.70
2.65	abdf	8.33
2.66	b	8.13
2.67	d	8.23
2.68	bd	8.21
2.69	c	4.20
2.70	b	8.51
2.71	c	8.49
2.72	c	8.52
2.73	c	10.46
2.74	d	10.47
2.75	b	10.32
2.76	d	9.5
2.77	d	10.3
2.78	b	10.4
2.79	a	10.5
2.80	c	9.40
2.81	c	9.34
2.82	ad	14.1
2.83	b	11.120
2.84	b	10.2
2.85	b	5.42
2.86	ae	5.28
2.87	d	4.6
2.88	d	2.7
2.89	a	4.13
2.90	d	2.6
2.91	a	4.55
2.92	b	2.4
2.93	ae	5.48
2.94	c	4.7
2.95	b	4.56
2.96	b	2.28
2.97	abd	8.56
2.98	b	4.52

Answers Section: 3

Book No		DSA No
3.1	c	11.138
3.2	b	11.141
3.3	c	11.96
3.4	a	11.99
3.5	c	11.95
3.6	c	11.116
3.7	c	8.10
3.8	c	9.18
3.9	c	9.19
3.10	c	9.20
3.11	c	11.115
3.12	b	9.26
3.13	d	9.30
3.14	c	5.32
3.15	a	7.13
3.16	a	11.108
3.17	ae	10.35
3.18	b	10.14
3.19	a	9.14
3.20	b	11.84
3.21	d	10.51
3.22	d	10.50
3.23	bef	10.49
3.24	ab	10.63
3.25	a	10.74
3.26	c	2.35
3.27	d	10.16
3.28	a	2.19
3.29	d	11.39
3.30	c	1.30
3.31	d	10.45
3.32	b	5.47
3.33	b	10.36
3.34	a	10.42
3.35	a	5.29
3.36	c	2.43
3.37	a	5.18
3.38	a	5.24
3.39	abe	5.69
3.40	ab	1.15
3.41	abcd	1.16
3.42	abcd	1.12
3.43	b	1.18
3.44	b	1.22
3.45	b	1.20
3.46	c	1.21
3.47	d	1.28
3.48	b	1.27
3.49	b	1.26
3.50	c	1.17
3.51	c	1.6
3.52	d	1.19
3.53	c	13.42
3.54	a	5.43
3.55	ace	5.7
3.56	cde	10.33
3.57	a	3.9
3.58	bf	5.26
3.59	d	6.68
3.60	a	8.6
3.61	c	8.8
3.62	a	3.81
3.63	a	11.4
3.64	d	11.7
3.65	b	11.57
3.66	b	11.98
3.67	a	5.22
3.68	c	4.28
3.69	d	3.10
3.70	c	6.51
3.71	d	5.41
3.72	b	2.42
3.73	d	2.41
3.74	c	2.40
3.75	c	8.16
3.76	d	10.71

Answers Section: 4

Book No		DSA No
4.1	c	1.1
4.2	abe	1.24
4.3	d	1.10
4.4	b	4.29
4.5	a	4.10
4.6	a	4.26
4.7	c	4.25
4.8	b	1.9
4.9	ac	6.21
4.10	c	6.20
4.11	a	6.58
4.12	b	7.22
4.13	ace	8.2
4.14	c	1.25
4.15	b	10.34
4.16	b	6.80
4.17	a	7.8
4.18	b	7.7
4.19	d	7.20
4.20	c	11.149
4.21	c	1.5
4.22	d	10.7
4.23	ace	4.11
4.24	d	8.12
4.25	b	5.34
4.26	d	7.19
4.27	d	7.18
4.28	c	2.33
4.29	c	8.1
4.30	b	2.9
4.31	c	5.74
4.32	c	2.31
4.33	b	7.16
4.34	b	6.83
4.35	b	6.61
4.36	c	6.22
4.37	b	6.5
4.38	c	6.63
4.39	b	6.84
4.40	b	11.27
4.41	a	5.17
4.42	b	11.97
4.43	b	10.41
4.44	c	1.29
4.45	a	10.61
4.46	c	10.20
4.47	a	10.21
4.48	c	11.142
4.49	b	11.143
4.50	d	8.5
4.51	a	11.130
4.52	c	11.86
4.53	d	11.87
4.54	c	11.88
4.55	c	11.92
4.56	b	11.89
4.57	a	11.90
4.58	a	5.44

Book No	Ans	DSA No
4.59	c	2.20
4.60	d	6.79
4.61	c	6.70
4.62	b	6.65
4.63	d	6.6
4.64	a	10.31
4.65	d	5.45
4.66	c	6.54
4.67	d	6.46
4.68	d	10.52
4.69	d	10.19
4.70	a	10.17
4.71	adf	10.8
4.72	d	10.18
4.73	d	6.48
4.74	a	6.55
4.75	d	6.18
4.76	c	6.45
4.77	ac	6.32
4.78	d	6.19
4.79	b	11.102
4.80	a	11.94
4.81	a	5.5
4.82	d	3.83
4.83	a	2.44
4.84	a	6.38
4.85	a	2.2
4.86	c	10.24
4.87	d	5.6
4.88	b	2.39
4.89	d	6.82
4.90	a	2.26
4.91	b	10.27
4.92	d	2.1
4.93	c	6.66
4.94	a	10.28
4.95	d	6.35
4.96	ae	6.67
4.97	a	2.27
4.98	c	2.3
4.99	a	10.58
4.100	d	10.55
4.101	b	10.60
4.102	b	6.60
4.103	d	1.34
4.104	d	6.62
4.105	a	10.57

Answers Section: 5

Book No	Ans	DSA No
5.1	abc	6.28
5.2	c	6.4
5.3	d	6.52
5.4	c	6.69
5.5	b	6.72
5.6	c	6.3
5.7	d	6.2
5.8	b	5.33
5.9	d	6.14
5.10	b	6.15

Book No	Ans	DSA No
5.11	d	6.16
5.12	c	5.20
5.13	a	6.36
5.14	b	5.14
5.15	c	6.43
5.16	d	6.11
5.17	c	6.10
5.18	c	5.4
5.19	c	6.23
5.20	c	6.29
5.21	ace	6.47
5.22	b	5.40
5.23	c	5.12
5.24	c	6.26
5.25	d	6.27
5.26	b	5.27
5.27	b	7.1
5.28	c	6.44
5.29	b	2.37
5.30	abd	6.33
5.31	d	2.38
5.32	b	6.31
5.33	de	2.36
5.34	d	6.73
5.35	c	5.19
5.36	c	6.53
5.37	a	6.50
5.38	b	6.49
5.39	a	2.12
5.40	d	5.30
5.41	d	6.57
5.42	c	7.15
5.43	b	7.27
5.44	b	5.15
5.45	a	5.16
5.46	c	5.35
5.47	b	7.4
5.48	a	2.30
5.49	d	7.6
5.50	a	7.14
5.51	b	7.5
5.52	a	2.45
5.53	cd	5.21
5.54	ac	7.25
5.55	b	2.22
5.56	c	5.9
5.57	b	7.10
5.58	bc	7.9
5.59	d	7.29
5.60	a	6.59

Answers Section: 6

Book No	Ans	DSA No
6.1	b	7.28
6.2	d	8.28
6.3	a	8.46
6.4	a	8.43
6.5	b	8.37
6.6	a	8.47
6.7	d	8.35
6.8	a	8.29

Book No	Ans	DSA No
6.9	bd	7.26
6.10	ab	1.14
6.11	c	8.60
6.12	c	13.63
6.13	cd	5.39
6.14	d	4.46
6.15	a	8.3
6.16	a	7.12
6.17	d	4.49
6.18	d	4.51
6.19	a	4.53
6.20	d	8.62
6.21	bdef	4.21
6.22	d	8.53
6.23	d	4.1
6.24	d	4.2
6.25	bd	4.50
6.26	b	4.22
6.27	a	4.15
6.28	d	4.47
6.29	a	4.48
6.30	d	4.23
6.31	ae	4.17
6.32	d	7.11
6.33	b	4.4
6.34	a	11.64
6.35	b	8.24
6.36	d	4.5
6.37	b	7.21
6.38	a	7.2
6.39	c	8.14
6.40	c	8.27
6.41	d	8.9
6.42	d	8.18
6.43	ce	8.26
6.44	ab	8.38
6.45	bd	8.39
6.46	acd	8.41
6.47	b	8.42
6.48	b	8.45
6.49	d	8.61
6.50	a	8.34
6.51	a	8.40
6.52	bc	4.3
6.53	bc	4.9
6.54	d	3.88
6.55	a	10.11
6.56	a	10.67
6.57	c	10.30
6.58	a	10.72
6.59	d	10.68
6.60	ade	3.90
6.61	abe	3.89
6.62	abd	10.38
6.63	a	10.37
6.64	bdef	10.9
6.65	ad	10.10
6.66	a	3.21
6.67	a	10.13
6.68	b	3.22
6.69	b	10.69

Book No	Ans	DSA No
6.70	b	10.40
6.71	c	8.31
6.72	a	8.30
6.73	ad	4.27

Answers Section: 7

Book No	Ans	DSA No
7.1	adef	9.1
7.2	adef	9.2
7.3	c	9.51
7.4	d	9.15
7.5	b	5.50
7.6	b	11.129
7.7	d	9.3
7.8	d	9.4
7.9	c	9.24
7.10	d	9.6
7.11	b	9.38
7.12	a	9.27
7.13	a	9.7
7.14	d	9.35
7.15	b	9.8
7.16	b	9.28
7.17	d	9.46
7.18	b	11.114
7.19	d	9.43
7.20	c	9.9
7.21	a	9.41
7.22	d	9.33
7.23	c	9.21
7.24	cdf	9.31
7.25	b	9.50

Answers Section: 8

Book No	Ans	DSA No
8.1	be	13.57
8.2	b	13.67
8.3	d	8.57
8.4	c	13.54
8.5	b	13.53
8.6	c	13.46
8.7	def	13.52
8.8	b	13.35
8.9	c	9.22
8.10	a	9.12
8.11	b	9.37
8.12	c	13.51
8.13	a	9.47
8.14	c	9.13
8.15	a	9.44
8.16	a	13.38
8.17	a	13.56
8.18	b	13.40
8.19	abe	13.4
8.20	b	13.3
8.21	ade	13.59
8.22	a	13.1
8.23	c	9.11
8.24	d	13.30
8.25	abe	13.11
8.26	acf	13.6

Book No	Ans	DSA No
8.27	b	6.30
8.28	bcde	13.2
8.29	c	13.15
8.30	d	9.39
8.31	b	13.19
8.32	a	13.5
8.33	a	13.7
8.34	c	6.76
8.35	a	13.60
8.36	abce	13.58
8.37	bde	13.32
8.38	b	12.3
8.39	ace	11.146
8.40	a	10.44
8.41	c	9.32
8.42	c	5.73
8.43	acd	11.83
8.44	d	11.81
8.45	d	10.66
8.46	b	9.29
8.47	b	9.42
8.48	c	11.82
8.49	c	10.54
8.50	c	10.53
8.51	a	10.39
8.52	c	5.25
8.53	c	13.33
8.54	b	5.38
8.55	a	13.48
8.56	abd	13.47
8.57	a	13.55
8.58	bdf	8.7
8.59	a	2.16
8.60	b	2.17

Answers Section: 9

Book No	Ans	DSA No
9.1	b	11.121
9.2	a	11.137
9.3	a	11.85
9.4	bdf	11.93
9.5	a	11.109
9.6	d	11.110
9.7	c	11.111
9.8	d	11.112
9.9	a	11.140
9.10	b	7.17
9.11	a	9.16
9.12	a	11.117
9.13	a	11.147
9.14	d	11.132
9.15	b	11.131
9.16	d	11.106
9.17	b	11.150
9.18	d	11.105
9.19	b	5.3
9.20	c	10.1
9.21	d	11.10
9.22	b	11.8
9.23	a	11.6
9.24	d	11.9

Book No		DSA No
9.25	b	11.5
9.26	a	11.3
9.27	a	11.2
9.28	b	10.12
9.29	d	11.11
9.30	c	11.21
9.31	d	11.1
9.32	c	11.22
9.33	d	11.127
9.34	a	11.124
9.35	c	11.100
9.36	d	11.119
9.37	d	11.31
9.38	c	11.30
9.39	b	11.135
9.40	b	11.25
9.41	c	11.13
9.42	b	11.20
9.43	a	11.18
9.44	c	11.17
9.45	c	11.16
9.46	d	11.15
9.47	a	11.14
9.48	d	11.29

Answers Section: 10

Book No		DSA No
10.1	a	11.36
10.2	b	11.59
10.3	c	11.56
10.4	c	11.55
10.5	acef	11.49
10.6	d	11.48
10.7	a	11.47
10.8	a	11.44
10.9	a	11.41
10.10	b	11.40
10.11	b	11.60
10.12	d	11.37
10.13	b	11.45
10.14	d	11.35
10.15	c	11.34
10.16	b	11.33
10.17	c	11.32
10.18	a	11.12
10.19	b	11.69
10.20	c	10.6
10.21	b	6.17
10.22	d	6.13
10.23	c	5.11
10.24	b	11.38
10.25	a	11.62
10.26	c	11.63
10.27	a	11.91
10.28	d	11.61
10.29	a	5.46
10.30	b	11.125
10.31	c	11.50
10.32	b	6.9
10.33	a	6.12
10.34	b	11.46
10.35	a	11.71
10.36	a	11.136
10.37	a	11.67
10.38	d	6.1
10.39	a	11.51
10.40	a	11.52
10.41	c	11.53
10.42	d	11.54
10.43	d	11.66
10.44	c	11.65
10.45	b	11.58
10.46	c	11.68
10.47	c	11.113
10.48	a	11.23
10.49	c	11.75
10.50	d	10.43
10.51	c	11.80
10.52	b	11.72
10.53	b	11.73
10.54	c	11.74
10.55	b	11.118
10.56	b	11.19
10.57	d	9.17
10.58	c	11.26
10.59	c	11.139
10.60	a	11.43
10.61	a	11.42
10.62	d	11.28
10.63	b	10.48
10.64	a	11.122
10.65	d	5.1
10.66	d	11.123
10.67	c	5.49
10.68	b	5.37
10.69	a	11.148
10.70	c	11.128
10.71	a	11.101
10.72	b	11.153
10.73	b	3.8
10.74	c	6.77
10.75	b	11.154
10.76	d	6.40
10.77	c	6.85
10.78	c	13.31
10.79	cd	5.2

Answers Section: 11

Book No		DSA No
11.1	b	12.17
11.2	d	12.8
11.3	b	12.7
11.4	c	12.1
11.5	c	12.13
11.6	b	12.16
11.7	c	12.6
11.8	c	12.18
11.9	abd	12.26
11.10	abf	12.19
11.11	bce	12.20
11.12	c	12.25
11.13	cd	12.15
11.14	d	12.11
11.15	bc	5.51
11.16	ab	12.9
11.17	d	6.74
11.18	c	12.5
11.19	be	12.4
11.20	b	5.54
11.21	bcdf	3.23
11.22	cde	3.53
11.23	d	13.45
11.24	ab	3.2
11.25	b	3.39
11.26	b	3.40
11.27	d	3.13
11.28	bef	3.4
11.29	cd	13.49
11.30	bc	3.27
11.31	ce	13.50
11.32	b	3.1
11.33	b	3.55
11.34	d	3.37
11.35	d	13.61
11.36	be	13.69
11.37	c	3.71
11.38	d	3.64
11.39	a	3.67
11.40	c	3.84
11.41	c	3.66
11.42	b	3.65
11.43	d	3.62
11.44	b	3.61
11.45	c	3.60
11.46	a	3.59
11.47	b	3.86
11.48	b	3.85
11.49	d	3.69
11.50	cd	13.25
11.51	def	13.10
11.52	acf	13.12
11.53	ae	13.13
11.54	c	13.28
11.55	d	13.41
11.56	abd	13.8
11.57	ace	13.9
11.58	acde	13.14
11.59	bc	13.16
11.60	cde	13.17
11.61	a	13.18
11.62	b	13.22
11.63	d	13.26
11.64	c	13.27
11.65	b	13.39
11.66	bde	13.21

Answers Section: 12

Book No		DSA No
12.1	c	12.17
12.2	cde	12.14
12.3	d	12.12
12.4	d	12.27
12.5	d	12.10
12.6	bd	12.22
12.7	d	12.23
12.8	a	12.24
12.9	d	6.81
12.10	d	6.56
12.11	b	12.2
12.12	b	12.28
12.13	c	3.7
12.14	abf	3.44
12.15	abf	3.3
12.16	abc	3.45
12.17	bdf	3.47
12.18	a	3.75
12.19	d	3.76
12.20	d	3.24
12.21	b	3.77
12.22	bcd	3.78
12.23	d	3.42
12.24	ae	3.16
12.25	acf	3.6
12.26	b	3.54
12.27	c	3.11
12.28	d	3.17
12.29	cd	3.80
12.30	d	3.12
12.31	abc	3.46
12.32	ab	3.74
12.33	ade	3.49
12.34	c	3.56
12.35	d	3.38
12.36	bdf	3.50
12.37	b	3.52
12.38	c	3.79
12.39	bd	14.6
12.40	d	3.25
12.41	b	3.57
12.42	a	3.15
12.43	bc	3.26
12.44	de	3.58
12.45	a	3.82
12.46	d	3.19
12.47	d	3.20
12.48	b	3.18
12.49	a	8.63
12.50	a	3.28
12.51	d	5.71
12.52	ac	1.11
12.53	a	5.36
12.54	a	6.75
12.55	a	3.31
12.56	a	2.47
12.57	c	3.39
12.58	bc	4.36
12.59	b	1.23
12.60	d	13.24
12.61	c	13.23
12.62	b	13.29
12.63	b	13.20
12.64	a	8.50
12.65	c	8.58
12.66	bd	8.22
12.67	d	3.51
12.68	d	3.48
12.69	ab	3.43
12.70	a	10.56
12.71	c	10.59
12.72	d	10.62
12.73	d	14.7
12.74	c	11.24
12.75	a	11.76
12.76	a	11.77
12.77	c	11.78
12.78	b	11.79
12.79	d	6.78
12.80	a	11.144
12.81	c	1.7
12.82	a	13.68
12.83	b	13.44
12.84	a	6.41
12.85	b	10.23
12.86	de	8.11
12.87	c	13.43
12.88	c	8.19
12.89	a	10.15
12.90	c	5.68
12.91	b	7.23
12.92	b	14.8
12.93	d	14.10
12.94	d	14.3
12.95	b	5.94
12.96	a	4.24
12.97	d	2.13
12.98	a	2.15
12.99	bcd	2.10
12.100	b	2.14
12.101	abe	2.11
12.102	d	1.33
12.103	c	6.64
12.104	d	5.90
12.105	c	1.31
12.106	d	5.13
12.107	a	11.156
12.108	d	2.25
12.109	a	7.3
12.110	d	5.31
12.111	a	1.32
12.112	b	6.71
12.113	b	2.8
12.114	c	2.5
12.115	d	8.17
12.116	a	5.10
12.117	c	1.3
12.118	d	1.4
12.119	bdf	1.2
12.120	b	7.24
12.121	ace	4.44
12.122	c	8.44
12.123	c	8.48
12.124	a	10.64
12.125	b	3.68
12.126	d	3.63

12.127	**d**	3.91
12.128	**b**	3.73
12.129	**d**	10.65
12.130	**b**	3.87
12.131	**a**	3.72
12.132	**d**	6.37
12.133	**b**	2.46
12.134	**c**	1.8
12.135	**d**	6.39
12.136	**cd**	8.4
12.137	**a**	2.32
12.138	**d**	10.73
12.139	**b**	9.23
12.140	**d**	9.45
12.141	**b**	11.107
12.142	**a**	13.34
12.143	**b**	9.25
12.144	**b**	9.49

1. Alertness

DSA	Book
1.1	4.1
1.2	12.119
1.3	12.117
1.4	12.118
1.5	4.21
1.6	3.51
1.7	12.81
1.8	12.134
1.9	4.8
1.10	4.3
1.11	12.52
1.12	3.42
1.13	1.39
1.14	6.10
1.15	3.40
1.16	3.41
1.17	3.50
1.18	3.43
1.19	3.52
1.20	3.45
1.21	3.46
1.22	3.44
1.23	12.59
1.24	4.2
1.25	4.14
1.26	3.49
1.27	3.48
1.28	3.47
1.29	4.44
1.30	3.30
1.31	12.105
1.32	12.111
1.33	12.102
1.34	4.103

2. Attitude

DSA	Book
2.1	4.92
2.2	4.85
2.3	4.98
2.4	2.92
2.5	12.114
2.6	2.90
2.7	2.88
2.8	12.113
2.9	4.30
2.10	12.99
2.11	12.101
2.12	5.39
2.13	12.97
2.14	12.100
2.15	12.98
2.16	8.59
2.17	8.60
2.18	2.18
2.19	3.28
2.20	4.59
2.21	1.6
2.22	5.55
2.23	2.13
2.24	2.12
2.25	12.108
2.26	4.90
2.27	4.97
2.28	2.96
2.29	2.20
2.30	5.48
2.31	4.32
2.32	12.137
2.33	4.28
2.34	2.27
2.35	3.26
2.36	5.33
2.37	5.29
2.38	5.31
2.39	4.88
2.40	3.74
2.41	3.73
2.42	3.72
2.43	3.36
2.44	4.83
2.45	5.52
2.46	12.133
2.47	12.56

3. Safety and your vehicle

DSA	Book
3.1	11.32
3.2	11.24
3.3	12.15
3.4	11.28
3.5	2.14
3.6	12.25
3.7	12.13
3.8	10.73
3.9	3.57
3.10	3.69
3.11	12.27
3.12	12.30
3.13	11.27
3.14	2.16
3.15	12.42
3.16	12.24
3.17	12.28
3.18	12.48
3.19	12.46
3.20	12.47
3.21	6.66
3.22	6.68
3.23	11.21
3.24	12.20
3.25	12.40
3.26	12.43
3.27	11.30
3.28	12.50
3.29	2.52
3.30	12.57
3.31	12.55
3.32	1.11
3.33	1.10
3.34	1.12
3.35	1.22
3.36	1.20
3.37	11.34
3.38	12.35
3.39	11.25
3.40	11.26
3.41	1.21
3.42	12.23
3.43	12.69
3.44	12.14
3.45	12.16
3.46	12.31
3.47	12.17
3.48	12.68
3.49	12.33
3.50	12.36
3.51	12.67
3.52	12.37
3.53	11.22
3.54	12.26
3.55	11.33
3.56	12.34
3.57	12.41
3.58	12.44
3.59	11.46
3.60	11.45
3.61	11.44
3.62	11.43
3.63	12.126
3.64	11.38
3.65	11.42
3.66	11.41
3.67	11.39
3.68	12.125
3.69	11.49
3.70	1.24
3.71	11.37
3.72	12.131
3.73	12.128
3.74	12.32
3.75	12.18
3.76	12.19
3.77	12.21
3.78	12.22
3.79	12.38
3.80	12.29
3.81	3.62
3.82	12.45
3.83	4.82
3.84	11.40
3.85	11.48
3.86	11.47
3.87	12.130
3.88	6.54
3.89	6.61
3.90	6.60
3.91	12.127

4. Safety margins

DSA	Book
4.1	6.23
4.2	6.24
4.3	6.52
4.4	6.33
4.5	6.36
4.6	2.87
4.7	2.94
4.8	2.2
4.9	6.53
4.10	4.5
4.11	4.23
4.12	2.63
4.13	2.89
4.14	2.44
4.15	6.27
4.16	2.46
4.17	6.31
4.18	2.42
4.19	2.43
4.20	2.69
4.21	6.21
4.22	6.26
4.23	6.30
4.24	12.96
4.25	4.7
4.26	4.6
4.27	6.73
4.28	3.68
4.29	4.4
4.30	2.51
4.31	2.47
4.32	2.50
4.33	2.54
4.34	2.53
4.35	2.56
4.36	12.58
4.37	2.57
4.38	2.58
4.39	2.59
4.40	2.60
4.41	2.49
4.42	2.48
4.43	2.55
4.44	12.121
4.45	2.62
4.46	6.14
4.47	6.28
4.48	6.29
4.49	6.17
4.50	6.25
4.51	6.18
4.52	2.98
4.53	6.19
4.54	2.61
4.55	2.91
4.56	2.95

5. Hazard awareness

DSA	Book
5.1	10.65
5.2	10.79
5.3	9.19
5.4	5.18
5.5	4.81
5.6	4.87
5.7	3.55
5.8	2.5
5.9	5.56
5.10	12.116
5.11	10.23
5.12	5.23
5.13	12.106
5.14	5.14
5.15	5.44
5.16	5.45
5.17	4.41
5.18	3.37
5.19	5.35
5.20	5.12
5.21	5.53
5.22	3.67
5.23	1.37
5.24	3.38
5.25	8.52
5.26	3.58
5.27	5.26
5.28	2.86
5.29	3.35
5.30	5.40
5.31	12.110
5.32	3.14
5.33	5.8
5.34	4.25
5.35	5.46
5.36	12.53
5.37	10.68
5.38	8.54
5.39	6.13
5.40	5.22
5.41	3.71
5.42	2.85
5.43	3.54
5.44	4.58
5.45	4.65
5.46	10.29
5.47	3.32
5.48	2.93
5.49	10.67
5.50	7.5
5.51	11.15
5.52	1.25
5.53	1.52
5.54	11.20
5.55	1.51
5.56	1.55
5.57	1.54
5.58	1.27
5.59	1.30
5.60	1.40
5.61	1.58
5.62	1.38
5.63	1.36
5.64	1.35
5.65	1.34
5.66	1.47
5.67	1.56
5.68	12.90
5.69	3.39
5.70	2.19
5.71	12.51
5.72	1.32
5.73	8.42
5.74	4.31
5.75	1.43
5.76	1.48
5.77	1.50
5.78	1.53
5.79	1.57
5.80	1.59
5.81	1.29
5.82	1.42
5.83	1.33
5.84	1.46
5.85	1.49
5.86	1.31
5.87	1.28
5.88	2.39
5.89	2.40
5.90	12.104
5.91	2.32
5.92	2.33
5.93	2.34
5.94	12.95

6. Vulnerable road users

DSA	Book
6.1	10.38
6.2	5.7
6.3	5.6
6.4	5.2
6.5	4.37
6.6	4.63
6.7	1.5
6.8	1.2
6.9	10.32
6.10	5.17
6.11	5.16
6.12	10.33
6.13	10.22
6.14	5.9
6.15	5.10
6.16	5.11
6.17	10.21
6.18	4.75
6.19	4.78

DSA	Book
6.20	4.10
6.21	4.9
6.22	4.36
6.23	5.19
6.24	1.8
6.25	1.9
6.26	5.24
6.27	5.25
6.28	5.1
6.29	5.20
6.30	8.27
6.31	5.32
6.32	4.77
6.33	5.30
6.34	1.1
6.35	4.95
6.36	5.13
6.37	12.132
6.38	4.84
6.39	12.135
6.40	10.76
6.41	12.84
6.42	1.3
6.43	5.15
6.44	5.28
6.45	4.76
6.46	4.67
6.47	5.21
6.48	4.73
6.49	5.38
6.50	5.37
6.51	3.70
6.52	5.3
6.53	5.36
6.54	4.66
6.55	4.74
6.56	12.10
6.57	5.41
6.58	4.11
6.59	5.60
6.60	4.102
6.61	4.35
6.62	4.104
6.63	4.38
6.64	12.103
6.65	4.62
6.66	4.93
6.67	4.96
6.68	3.59
6.69	5.4
6.70	4.61
6.71	12.112
6.72	5.5
6.73	5.34
6.74	11.17
6.75	12.54
6.76	8.34
6.77	10.74
6.78	12.79
6.79	4.60
6.80	4.16
6.81	12.9
6.82	4.89
6.83	4.34
6.84	4.39
6.85	10.77

7. Other types of vehicle

DSA	Book
7.1	5.27
7.2	6.38
7.3	12.109
7.4	5.47
7.5	5.51
7.6	5.49
7.7	4.18
7.8	4.17
7.9	5.58
7.10	5.57
7.11	6.32
7.12	6.16
7.13	3.15
7.14	5.50
7.15	5.42
7.16	4.33
7.17	9.10
7.18	4.27
7.19	4.26
7.20	4.19
7.21	6.37
7.22	4.12
7.23	12.91
7.24	12.120
7.25	5.54
7.26	6.9
7.27	5.43
7.28	6.1
7.29	5.59

8. Vehicle handling

DSA	Book
8.1	4.29
8.2	4.13
8.3	6.15
8.4	12.136
8.5	4.50
8.6	3.60
8.7	8.58
8.8	3.61
8.9	6.41
8.10	3.7
8.11	12.86
8.12	4.24
8.13	2.66
8.14	6.39
8.15	2.26
8.16	3.75
8.17	12.115
8.18	6.42
8.19	12.88
8.20	2.28
8.21	2.68
8.22	12.66
8.23	2.67
8.24	6.35
8.25	2.45
8.26	6.43
8.27	6.40
8.28	6.2
8.29	6.8
8.30	6.72
8.31	6.71
8.32	2.29
8.33	2.65
8.34	6.50
8.35	6.7
8.36	2.24
8.37	6.5
8.38	6.44
8.39	6.45
8.40	6.51
8.41	6.46
8.42	6.47
8.43	6.4
8.44	12.122
8.45	6.48
8.46	6.3
8.47	6.6
8.48	12.123
8.49	2.71
8.50	12.64
8.51	2.70
8.52	2.72
8.53	6.22
8.54	2.22
8.55	2.21
8.56	2.97
8.57	8.3
8.58	12.65
8.59	2.23
8.60	6.11
8.61	6.49
8.62	6.20
8.63	12.49

9. Motorway rules

DSA	Book
9.1	7.1
9.2	7.2
9.3	7.7
9.4	7.8
9.5	2.76
9.6	7.10
9.7	7.13
9.8	7.15
9.9	7.20
9.10	1.41
9.11	8.23
9.12	8.10
9.13	8.14
9.14	3.19
9.15	7.4
9.16	9.11
9.17	10.57
9.18	3.8
9.19	3.9
9.20	3.10
9.21	7.23
9.22	8.9
9.23	12.139
9.24	7.9
9.25	12.143
9.26	3.12
9.27	7.12
9.28	7.16
9.29	8.46
9.30	3.13
9.31	7.24
9.32	8.41
9.33	7.22
9.34	2.81
9.35	7.14
9.36	2.30
9.37	8.11
9.38	7.11
9.39	8.30
9.40	2.80
9.41	7.21
9.42	8.47
9.43	7.19
9.44	8.15
9.45	12.140
9.46	7.17
9.47	8.13
9.48	2.37
9.49	12.144
9.50	7.25
9.51	7.3

10. Rules of the road

DSA	Book
10.1	9.20
10.2	2.84
10.3	2.77
10.4	2.78
10.5	2.79
10.6	10.20
10.7	4.22
10.8	4.71
10.9	6.64
10.10	6.65
10.11	6.55
10.12	9.28
10.13	6.67
10.14	3.18
10.15	12.89
10.16	3.27
10.17	4.70
10.18	4.72
10.19	4.69
10.20	4.46
10.21	4.47
10.22	2.7
10.23	12.85
10.24	4.86
10.25	1.4
10.26	1.7
10.27	4.91
10.28	4.94
10.29	2.25
10.30	6.57
10.31	4.64
10.32	2.75
10.33	3.56
10.34	4.15
10.35	3.17
10.36	3.33
10.37	6.63
10.38	6.62
10.39	8.51
10.40	6.70
10.41	4.43
10.42	3.34
10.43	10.50
10.44	8.40
10.45	3.31
10.46	2.73
10.47	2.74
10.48	10.63
10.49	3.23
10.50	3.22
10.51	3.21
10.52	4.68
10.53	8.50
10.54	8.49
10.55	4.100
10.56	12.70
10.57	4.105
10.58	4.99
10.59	12.71
10.60	4.101
10.61	4.45
10.62	12.72
10.63	3.24
10.64	12.124
10.65	12.129
10.66	8.45
10.67	6.56
10.68	6.59
10.69	6.69
10.70	2.8
10.71	3.76
10.72	6.58
10.73	12.138
10.74	3.25
10.75	2.1

11. Road and traffic signs

DSA	Book
11.1	9.31
11.2	9.27
11.3	9.26
11.4	3.63
11.5	9.25
11.6	9.23
11.7	3.64
11.8	9.22
11.9	9.24
11.10	9.21
11.11	9.29
11.12	10.18
11.13	9.41
11.14	9.47
11.15	9.46
11.16	9.45
11.17	9.44
11.18	9.43
11.19	10.56
11.20	9.42
11.21	9.30
11.22	9.32
11.23	10.48
11.24	12.74
11.25	9.40
11.26	10.58
11.27	4.40
11.28	10.62
11.29	9.48
11.30	9.38
11.31	9.37
11.32	10.17
11.33	10.16
11.34	10.15
11.35	10.14
11.36	10.1
11.37	10.12
11.38	10.24
11.39	3.29
11.40	10.10
11.41	10.9
11.42	10.61
11.43	10.60
11.44	10.8
11.45	10.13
11.46	10.34
11.47	10.7
11.48	10.6
11.49	10.5
11.50	10.31
11.51	10.39
11.52	10.40
11.53	10.41
11.54	10.42
11.55	10.4
11.56	10.3
11.57	3.65

DSA	Book
11.58	10.45
11.59	10.2
11.60	10.11
11.61	10.28
11.62	10.25
11.63	10.26
11.64	6.34
11.65	10.44
11.66	10.43
11.67	10.37
11.68	10.46
11.69	10.19
11.70	2.64
11.71	10.35
11.72	10.52
11.73	10.53
11.74	10.54
11.75	10.49
11.76	12.75
11.77	12.76
11.78	12.77
11.79	12.78
11.80	10.51
11.81	8.44
11.82	8.48
11.83	8.43
11.84	3.20
11.85	9.3
11.86	4.52
11.87	4.53
11.88	4.54
11.89	4.56
11.90	4.57
11.91	10.27
11.92	4.55
11.93	9.4
11.94	4.80
11.95	3.5
11.96	3.3
11.97	4.42
11.98	3.66
11.99	3.4
11.100	9.35
11.101	10.71
11.102	4.79
11.103	2.10
11.104	2.9
11.105	9.18
11.106	9.16
11.107	12.141
11.108	3.16
11.109	9.5
11.110	9.6
11.111	9.7
11.112	9.8
11.113	10.47
11.114	7.18
11.115	3.11
11.116	3.6
11.117	9.12
11.118	10.55
11.119	9.36
11.120	2.83
11.121	9.1
11.122	10.64
11.123	10.66
11.124	9.34
11.125	10.30
11.126	2.3
11.127	9.33
11.128	10.70
11.129	7.6
11.130	4.51
11.131	9.15
11.132	9.14
11.133	2.15
11.134	2.17
11.135	9.39
11.136	10.36
11.137	9.2
11.138	3.1
11.139	10.59
11.140	9.9
11.141	3.2
11.142	4.48
11.143	4.49
11.144	12.80
11.145	2.11
11.146	8.39
11.147	9.13
11.148	10.69
11.149	4.20
11.150	9.17
11.151	2.6
11.152	2.36
11.153	10.72
11.154	10.75
11.155	2.4
11.156	12.107

12. Documents

DSA	Book
12.1	11.4
12.2	12.11
12.3	8.38
12.4	11.19
12.5	11.18
12.6	11.7
12.7	11.3
12.8	11.2
12.9	11.16
12.10	12.5
12.11	11.14
12.12	12.3
12.13	11.5
12.14	12.2
12.15	11.13
12.16	11.6
12.17	11.1
12.18	11.8
12.19	11.10
12.20	11.11
12.21	1.26
12.22	12.6
12.23	12.7
12.24	12.8
12.25	11.12
12.26	11.9
12.27	12.4
12.28	12.12
12.29	12.1

13. Accidents

DSA	Book
13.1	8.22
13.2	8.28
13.3	8.20
13.4	8.19
13.5	8.32
13.6	8.26
13.7	8.33
13.8	11.56
13.9	11.57
13.10	11.51
13.11	8.25
13.12	11.52
13.13	11.53
13.14	11.58
13.15	8.29
13.16	11.59
13.17	11.60
13.18	11.61
13.19	8.31
13.20	12.63
13.21	11.66
13.22	11.62
13.23	12.61
13.24	12.60
13.25	11.50
13.26	11.63
13.27	11.64
13.28	11.54
13.29	12.62
13.30	8.24
13.31	10.78
13.32	8.37
13.33	8.53
13.34	12.142
13.35	8.8
13.36	2.35
13.37	2.38
13.38	8.16
13.39	11.65
13.40	8.18
13.41	11.55
13.42	3.53
13.43	12.87
13.44	12.83
13.45	11.23
13.46	8.6
13.47	8.56
13.48	8.55
13.49	11.29
13.50	11.31
13.51	8.12
13.52	8.7
13.53	8.5
13.54	8.4
13.55	8.57
13.56	8.17
13.57	8.1
13.58	8.36
13.59	8.21
13.60	8.35
13.61	11.35
13.62	1.45
13.63	6.12
13.64	1.44
13.65	2.41
13.66	2.31
13.67	8.2
13.68	12.82
13.69	11.36

14. Vehicle loading

DSA	Book
14.1	2.82
14.2	1.14
14.3	12.94
14.4	1.13
14.5	1.18
14.6	12.39
14.7	12.73
14.8	12.92
14.9	1.15
14.10	12.93
14.11	1.17
14.12	1.16
14.13	1.23
14.14	1.19